LOSING

SOCIAL INTELLECT

Fundamental Awareness
in Economics and Politics

BOOK ONE

LOSING
SOCIAL
INTELLECT

The core reason behind the troubles in
Free Market Economy and Democracy

SALIH REISOGLU

Book One published in 2024

ISBN 979-8-9861604-8-1

Table of Contents

INTRODUCTION

The *Western Social Order* based on *Free Market Economy* and *Democracy* was taken to be the best among all the options after the fall of the Soviet Republics and their social order by the end of the 20th century. This view was challenged in 2008 when the economic system almost collapsed in the western world, but what has happened was naively thought to be a temporary crisis. Unfortunately, it was not.

A Tale Of Two Johns

John Junior is 25 years old. He has great plans for the future. He will take his last final exam this afternoon and will receive his master's degree from his university afterwards. Tomorrow morning, he will have an interview with the company he has been dreaming of working for, and expects to be offered a job. And tomorrow night he will meet his girlfriend to celebrate her birthday, during which he will propose to her. Everything is planned to perfection. A bright future is his. Dreaming of all these while walking to the campus, he fails to see a misplaced brick, steps on it, falls and breaks his arm and hits his head. In the ambulance, on the way to hospital, semi-consciously, he realizes that he can neither take his last exam today nor take the interview with the company tomorrow. He cannot even meet his girlfriend for her birthday, for which she will definitely have a broken heart. Everything turned upside down.

His medical examination revealed that hitting his head caused no serious problem. Only his arm required a medical treatment, which will be over within a month. His conscience regained, he gets a medical report and contacts his university to take the exam on a further date, calls the company and delays the interview for a couple weeks, and explains the accident to his girlfriend and receives a warm reply in return. A few weeks later, his arm bandage is removed, all problems are solved, and *everything is back to normal again.*

In a *short time*, and after a couple of *well-known treatments*, John Junior survived his first *unexpected catastrophic event*, also known as a *crisis*.

John Senior is 50 years old. He has been overweight and heavily smoking for decades. One day he had a serious heart attack. Everything has turned upside down. His treatment will be much complicated and will take much longer. Even if he is lucky to survive eventually, his life will *never be the same again*. He has to change his lifestyle completely, will need to lose weight, live on a healthy diet, should not undergo much stress, quit smoking and exercise regularly.

John Senior has faced an *outburst of accumulated structural damage*, whose arrival can be *forecasted beforehand* as a *high probability event*, even though the exact timing can not be known.

In economics and politics, societies face both *crises* and *outbursts of accumulated structural damages*. Unfortunately, they mostly fail to differentiate between the two, and thus fail to diagnose the real reason and apply the appropriate cure in time.

What has happened in 2008 ?

What is used to be called the 2008 crisis was actually the inevitable outburst of decades of accumulated structural damages in the western social order. Corporations gained power and mastered the art of lobbying to misguide both the regulators and the politicians to their own interest, at the expense of the rest of the society. Relaxing regulations, resulting in a decrease in competition and an increase in monopolization on the supply side of both goods and jobs, has increased corporate profits at the expense of both the consumer and the labour. Globalization transferred wealth from the advanced country unqualified labour towards the developing country labour, while making global corporations of the advanced countries richer. Automation increased efficiency to transfer further wealth from labour to capital. Economic Inequality rose to excessive levels within western societies. Demand is kept alive by increasing the indebtedness of the consumers up to unsustainable levels. Unfortunately, voters failed to counterbalance those developments. On the one hand, the inherent tendency of unregulated free markets to decrease competition was too old and moved too slowly. On the other hand, the phenomenon of globalization and automation were too new and moved too fast. Both escaped the *social awareness* of the society, and thus, the *society's political reaction on the years to the crisis was too weak and too wrong.* Naturally came the perfect storm.

The Last Chance Before The Point Of No Return

What happened in 2008 was not an unexpected temporary crisis, but an outburst of accumulated structural damages. All the unprecedented actions taken in the following fifteen years were just trying to cure the symptoms on the surface, never recognizing never admitting never treating the real cause.

Every passing day the world gets more integrated and more complex. Social Intellect, if it has ever existed in the past, gets comparatively weaker and weaker, with no signs of recovery.

And as long as Social Intellect remains inadequate, the structural damages will only accumulate further and get worse. So now may be the last chance for a change – before the Western Social Order is ruined irrevocably.

The Rising Pace Of Social Change

The pace of social change can be thought as the cumulative amount of developments in the economic, political and social environment, amplified by the accompanying scientific and technological progress, within a certain time period.

The rise in this pace in the recent decades brings out significant consequences. First, societies *lose their Social Intellect relative to the complexity of the world* (in simple terms, lose their ability to understand the economic and political environment) *ever faster than before.* Second, the higher rate of change in the social environment amplifies the heterogeneity of the society, which in turn reveals the weaknesses of the economic and political systems much clearer than before.

As the pace of social change is rising, each surfacing trouble carries the potential to turn into a catastrophe much faster than before and thus threaten the stability of the social order, and therefore the societies do not have the luxury to waste time with the wrong questions and irrelevant answers any more.

The Irresistible Attraction of Easy But Wrong Answers

When individuals face difficult problems, they prefer to fool themselves by looking for unrealistically fast and easy solutions, rather than going for the difficult but real one.

Similarly, in an economic and political context, societies mostly fail to diagnose the primary problem which will persist and even worsen in the long run when left to its own devices. And even in the cases where they diagnose correctly, rather than targeting the core reason behind the problem and investing the required time and effort to generate a real and sustainable solution, they prefer to look for a short-term solution that is fast and easy, but of course, wrong. Similarly, societies don't like those people around who talk about hard and painful solutions for the long-term, but they just look for somebody to propose an easy solution, that will at least postpone the problem to a distant future, only to hit them back as a much stronger and grave one sometime later, and usually much earlier than expected. A classic case of inadequate Social Intellect, as old as the human race.

The society, as the ultimate decision maker, can not find the right answers unless it asks the right questions first. In other words, to find the real remedies, it needs to focus on *the real troubles behind the advertised ones, none of which will be simple*. Unfortunately, *none of the remedies will be fast or easy either.*

The Fine Art Of Economic And Political Management

Management of economics and politics is the fine art of bringing out the optimal balance between contradicting opinions, all having their correct and incorrect arguments. Successful management is blending the strengths of each while avoiding their weaknesses as much as possible. Easy to say, extremely difficult to achieve.

It is commonly accepted that the optimal answer does not lie at any of the extremes, but a balanced approach is the best in most cases. However, the critical word here is "optimal" which can never be defined clearly in social matters. In economics and politics, which are based mainly on the behaviour of the human variable, the optimal has to be determined by the society.

The *success of the decision*, and thus the *success of its outcome*, depends mainly on the *intellectual level of the ultimate decision maker*, thus that of the *society* in a democracy. As the society gets more intellectual, it not only gets perfectly aware of the need to find a balance between the extremes, but it also enhances its ability to decide the optimal mix of the balance.

To make matters harder, the optimal balance depends on the specific conditions of each society at any given time. *There is no definite optimal balance on any issue that is valid for every society at every time.* Each society has to find its own optimal balance and manage it actively through time as conditions change. Copying from the past, even if it is the society's own past, will not help. Similarly, neither copying the optimal balance of another society, nor asserting its own optimal balance to another society is a bright idea.

On every issue discussed in the books in this series, all independent of any specific society or individual, I will try to reveal the critical issues to be taken into consideration in the search for an optimal balance at any specific place and time, rather than desperately trying to give a non-existent definite answer spanning all places and times.

It All Starts With Politics

The state casts a strong shadow on economics. And the state is run by the politicians, preferably those elected by the society, and thus, politics and economics are heavily integrated. Therefore, if the political system fails, the economic system has no choice but to fail sooner or later. The trouble is that, *the failure of the political system usually goes unnoticed until the failure of the economic system becomes clear*. Even worse, in most cases, the society still falls short of realising that *if something has gone wrong with economics, most probably something has been going wrong with politics way before that, and therefore, the economic system can not be cured unless the political system is cured first.*

Trying to solve economic troubles while political ones are standing still will be a waste of time. Societies need to start to cure the politics side preferably before, or at least simultaneously, with the economics side.

The Scope Of The Discussion

In economics and politics, everything is dependent on almost everything else, but it is impossible to examine such a complex system of relations by considering all variables simultaneously. Therefore, first the main pieces of the puzzle will be examined one by one, through the books in this series, and when all the pieces are complete by the end of the series, the full picture will emerge.

Losing Social Intellect, the first book in the series, focuses on Social Intellect[1] and its vitality for the two pillars of our Social Order, namely Free Market Economy and Democracy. The issues common to both pillars will be discussed in Chapters 1, 2 and 6, and when separate viewpoints are required for each pillar, the economics view will be discussed in Chapter 3, and the political ones in Chapters 4, 5 and 7.

NO SPECIFIC SOCIETY OR PERSON IS TARGETED, BUT ALL ARE COVERED

Although no countries or names are mentioned, the primary focus of the discussions in this series will seem to be on US, UK and the other economically advanced West European countries. However, the discussions, analyses and potential remedies mentioned in the books can be applied to any society that exercises a Free Market Economy and Democracy.

THE STYLE OF THE BOOK

Thanks to the free flow of information and the availability of a huge supply of it, and the new attention attracters growing exponentially within the digital media, most of us now have ultra short spans of attention. Messages are expected to be given too short, accompanied with the risk to be misunderstood even if they are right. In line with this practice of the 21st century, there is no sense in repeating the already-known, so I will just concentrate on what is wrong or missing, and how to cure it, carefully choosing every single word. To respect the time and to keep the attention of the reader, I will make all arguments as sharp and as short as possible.

I will therefore request the readers *to read between the lines* whenever necessary, *to integrate the pieces of the puzzle* as they read through the books in this series, and *to adopt the conclusions to their own societies*.

Chapter 1 : SOCIAL INTELLECT

1.1   What Is Social Intellect ?

The Good, The Bad, And The Innocent

In his poems *Innocence and Experience*, English poet William Blake tells that we are all born innocent. And when we are innocent, we are nothing but innocent – neither good, nor bad. Only when we get experienced, we leave our state of innocence. And only at that stage, we can choose to be good or bad. His powerful insight keeps its validity from then to eternity, and will shed light to our discussion on Social Intellect.

Children are all born physically weak, mentally naive and innocent. As they grow up, they get physically stronger, to become physically-adults. As their brain develops, they become mentally more capable, and in time, as they learn and experience their environment and the society they live in, they turn into mentally-adults. The crucial issue here is that, getting aged is a necessary but not sufficient condition to become mentally-adult. What really drives the process is learning and experiencing the world around them.

And when this learning and experiencing process is defined as the key to becoming mentally-adult, it follows that being mentally-child versus mentally-adult is not of black and white clarity, but there is a spectrum of shades in between, as this process is highly variable from person to person.

SOCIAL INTELLECT

From the perspective of economics and politics, the concepts of intellectually-child versus intellectually-adult can now be introduced. It is easy to guess that, independent of their age, people who did not have enough of a chance to get a basic education or much of an experience due to lack of exposure to different environments can be considered as intellectually-children. But it gets more complicated beyond that. Very many people get a good education, concentrate working on a specific subject, and become valuable experts on their areas of interest, such as a doctor or an engineer. Unfortunately, even such deep expertise does not necessarily mean that they have learnt and experienced enough on the social sciences that drive their relation and more importantly their social contribution to the society as political and economic participants.

What counts as intellect from an economic and political perspective is *Social Intellect*, which *is a balanced blend of intelligence, social education, social experience and social awareness*. Being intellectually-adult, therefore, is defined as being educated and experienced in *social sciences* that improve our *awareness* of the social environment around us, both as a political participant (at least as a voter) and as an economic participant (at least as a consumer and a supplier of labour) in the society. It naturally follows that *the ratio of the intellectually-adults in a society is the primary determinant of how good the political and economic systems of the society develop and function.*

Social Education & Awareness

PROFESSIONAL EXPERTISE IS NOT SOCIAL EDUCATION

Societies and individuals try their best to invest in education targeting professional expertise in many specific fields, and produce many experts who add value to the society and increase its welfare, in addition to making a good career and money for themselves, and all these are fine.

Unfortunately, *such professional education is not social education, and does not make an individual an intellectually-adult*. One may be a rocket scientist or a brain surgeon, but may still lack the proper social education that will create any social awareness. Social Intellect is not relevant to the existence or non-existence of professional expertise.

If the Social Intellect of a society is not adequate to run its economic and political systems properly, eventually an economic and political system failure will come and wipe out the gains created through investing in professional expertise. It is amazing to see how societies fail to realize that the experts created by the current education system can only create value for the society and for themselves if and only if they work in an economic and political system that gives them the opportunity to succeed in the long run. Otherwise, their expertise and efforts will be partially or completely wasted within a failing system. Therefore, each society must first develop its Social Intellect through a heavy investment in social education, before targeting to increase its members' professional expertise.

Unfortunately, although the current education systems may be good in eventually creating experts in ever-more-focused narrow fields, they fail to supply any social education to the society in general. And the societies wonder why their economic and political systems keep failing.

SCOPE OF SOCIAL EDUCATION

Social Education must span the basics of the primary social sciences of politics, economics, finance, law and sociology, to enable each individual to understand and to evaluate the dynamics of Free Market Economy and Democracy within a society. Only after getting such basic social education, followed by a real-life social experience, an individual can attain social awareness, and can be considered as an intellectually-adult. Otherwise, he will remain intellectually-childish for a lifetime.

It is of crucial importance to clarify that, the aim of social education is not, and can not be, to create an economics or politics expert out of each individual. All that is required of social education is to make each member of the society intellectual enough to be able to understand and evaluate the analysis of the real experts in social sciences, so that they can stay aware of the environment and make rational choices as consumers and voters.

SOCIAL AWARENESS

Social awareness is the continuous process of spending time and effort to observe and understand the developments in economics and politics within and out of the society. Therefore, an initial social education and accumulated social experience are necessary but not enough, but access to complete and correct information on the developments and to the analyses of the experts are also required. All these will be discussed in detail in the coming chapters.

1.2   Why Is Social Intellect Important ?

The Trouble With The Driver

If a car is crashed into a wall, unless the car has a major mechanical problem, it is not the car's fault, but the driver's. Similarly, when economic or political systems fail, as they sometimes do, it does not necessarily show that there is something wrong with the system. The problem may actually be with the driver, namely the consumer or the voter, for not being intellectual enough to make the system work.

To put more openly, if the free market is not working, the problem is primarily with the consumer, for not knowing what to demand, because the supplier responds to the demand of the consumer to sell his product. If the political system is not working, the primary problem is with the voter, for not knowing what is good for him, because the politician responds to the demand of the voter to stay in power. Therefore, contrary to the common belief, the main troubles in Free Market Economy and Democracy stem primarily from the inadequacy of the Social Intellect of the society, rather than the structural problems in the systems.

Taking the car analogy, advanced technologies enable never ending developments in both increasing the performance and decreasing the risks in driving. Still, however advanced a car may become, as long as the driver does not know how to drive properly, sooner or later he will have an accident.

Similarly, it makes sense to try to improve the economic and political systems as much as possible, however, the scope of possible can not reach the level of perfection such that these systems will work independent of the intellectual level of the driver, namely the consumer and the voter. Therefore, to improve the society's welfare, and to increase the sustainability of its economic and political systems, the intellectual level of the society has to be increased as much as possible as soon as possible.

The Role Of Social Intellect In Our Social Order

Every individual lives as a member of a society, and therefore plays the roles of both a consumer and a supplier of labour in the economy, and a voter in the political system. Thus, the individual interacts with the society, such that, not only the society effects his personal welfare, but his behaviour in these roles effect the welfare of the society as well. He is therefore assumed to have adequate social intellect to enable him to act rationally in making his economic and political decisions.

A MATTER OF ALLOCATION OF RESOURCES

In both politics and economics, demand and supply meet to form the equilibrium desired by the society. In economics the subject is the availability and pricing of goods and services, in politics it is rule making (legislation) and governance (execution). Within this macro picture, each individual plays his micro role. On the demand side, each individual acts as a consumer and a voter. On the supply side, in economics, he acts as some sort of supplier of physical or mental labour, and in politics he may act as a politician.

The macro-equilibrium in both economics and politics forms through a chain of interactions between the individual and the society. *Each individual has personal demand preferences as a consumer and a voter, that are primarily shaped by his Social Intellect.* Individual demands add up to create the society's macro-demand. In turn, the macro-supply of the society forms in reaction to that macro-demand, and each individual adjusts his personal micro-supply to fit into somewhere within that macro-supply. And through this chain reaction the overall resource allocation within the society emerges.

RATIONALITY AND OPTIMAL ALLOCATION OF RESOURCES

Economic and political theory assumes that the individual will act *rationally*, and by doing so, he will enable the *optimal allocation of the society's resources such that the society's welfare will be maximised*. Reading backwards, if due to the lack of adequate Social Intellect the individuals make irrational choices, then the society's limited resources will be misplaced and thus wasted, and the welfare of the society will decline.

To appreciate the scope and thus the importance of this observation, it will help to clarify what is meant by resources. One easy to guess component of the society's resources is the physical ones. These not only include the natural resources, but also cover labour, thus the physical capacity of a society's human resources. Another easy to guess component is financial resources. But more important are the scientific and technical resources, including the accumulated know-how within the society. And the most important is the mental capacity of the human resources of the society. The society's welfare will change one way or another depending on where and how these limited resources are allocated. The more intellectual the society gets, the better will be this allocation and thus the higher will be the society's welfare[2].

The concept of allocation of resources does not only refer to micro-level allocations, but more critically, refers to macro-level allocations. For instance, the society needs to decide whether scientific research or entertainment should have a higher priority in allocating its financial resources. Or, whether the best mental resources of the society, namely their brightest minds, should be primarily allocated to private financial sector or to politics and the state. There are very many dimensions among which the resources of the society have to be distributed, and the appropriate allocation will change over time and under different conditions. However, the critical issue here is that, the society's decisions regarding all the macro and micro level allocations should be made rationally at all times.

ON ACTING RATIONALLY

At this point it becomes critical to define what is rational. Contrary to the classical thinking, *rational does not necessarily mean absolutely logical.* Adding emotional considerations to the decision making process does not make it irrational. *Emotional decisions can also be rational* under certain circumstances, such as when they make the individual or the society feel better or happier. However, when an action makes neither logical nor emotional sense, it can then be considered irrational.

For instance, consider a simple case where you have worked hard to earn $100. One logical and rational move is to spend it for yourself. Another is to save it for the future. An emotional but still rational move may be to give it to somebody you know who needs it much more than you do, if it makes you happier than spending for yourself. However, tearing or burning the $100 banknote is irrational – as its value will be lost without any use to anybody.

Another simple example is what happens if you are carrying an umbrella and it starts to rain. A logical and rational move can be opening up the umbrella to protect yourself from the rain. An emotional and still rational move can be giving it to someone nearby who is in weaker health than you are and thus more vulnerable under rainy conditions. However, carrying the umbrella closed is irrational – as it has no use to anybody.

Therefore, there can be logical dimensions and emotional dimensions that can be taken into consideration while making rational decisions. And thus, in many cases there can be more than one rational choice. However, this does not mean that all choices are rational. Some choices are simply irrational, and having adequate Social Intellect enables the elimination of these irrational choices that harm the society's welfare most.

RATIONALITY AND CAUSATION

Causation simply refers to the chain of events from the reason(s) to the particular result. Understanding causation, therefore, refers to analysing and recognising the causes behind a certain outcome. In a world that becomes ever more complex every passing day, understanding causations are becoming more and more of a challenge for each individual. And once an individual starts to fail in understanding causations, it will be impossible for him to differentiate the rational from the irrational.

It easily follows that, the intellectually-childish will spectacularly fail on understanding causations in many ways. And it is easy to guess that, they will either fail to see many of the existing causations, or worse, will see some non-existent causations behind the economic and political developments. But the worst is that, they can be *manipulated to believe in non-existent causations and act accordingly, mostly against their own interests, to serve the economic or political interests of the others.*

Many common simple cases can be found in economics. An individual, as a consumer, can be made to believe that a certain product, say a non-prescription drug, will be beneficial to his health, while it is actually useless or even harmful, but just makes the producer richer. Or, on a more macro basis, he can be made to believe that a certain economic policy will benefit him, but he will actually be hurt by that policy in the longer run while some others will be improving their own financial wellbeing as a result of that policy.

A more dangerous case can be found in politics. An individual, as a voter, can be made to believe that there is an imaginary terrible outcome to fear on the horizon, with an irrelevant cause, to prevent which, he should vote for the populist politician – a very convenient case for the politicians who have no real promise to improve the welfare of the individual or the society.

Free markets and Democracy assume that each individual will act rationally – implicitly assuming he can judge causation relations properly. But as the world becomes more complex, everything starts to effect or be effected by many other things, and causations become extremely difficult to spot unless an individual's Social Intellect is high enough. And if he can't differentiate what is rational and what is not, which is a common case in real life practise, then he can not act rationally even if he wants to. Therefore, *for the intellectually-children the real problem is not the lack of goodwill to make the right choice, but the lack of the ability to distinguish the rational from the irrational.*

WHEN CHILDREN MEET ADULTS

Integrating Blake's viewpoint to our definitions, we can say that *the intellectually-children remain to be innocent.* As a consumer and a voter, even though they do not wish to do so, they just make too many mistakes in their economic and political judgements, or easily misguided by others to act in a manner to serve the mis-guiders' interests rather than their own. To take it further, even if they wish and try to do the right thing, the intellectually-children will probably lack the ability to properly see the correct causality relation between their actions and the consequences of those actions, thus may end up with just the opposite outcomes of their initial intentions.

And to make matters worse, not all the intellectually-adults are good guys from heavens, but some, who we will define as *Cheaters* in the coming sections, choose to serve their own interests at the expense of others in the society, even if that may require playing unfair, unethical or even illegal. And to serve their own purpose, they will not hesitate to misguide the intellectually-children.

Consider an analogy on children. Assume one person offers sweet candies to the children, which is fun in the short run but bad for them in the long run. Another person offers vitamins, which are tasteless and not fun, but beneficial in the long run. Which offer will the children choose? And which would have been the right choice? The important observation here is that, in this case, the candy producers will support *the children's right-to-choose-freely without any third party intervention, even though they have not yet become adults to make rational decisions*, knowing that the children will act in the way that will benefit the candy producer against their own interest. In this simple example, only time is required for the children to grow up and survive the trap. In real life, unfortunately, time alone does not solve any problems.

If a society is dominated by the intellectually-children, these innocent people, and thus both the economic and the political system of the society, is left to the mercy of the few intellectually-adults, among which the Cheaters can easily discredit the good guys and dominate the system, as making the innocent crowds believe in fast-simple-but-false promises is much easier than explaining complicated issues with rather painful long-term solutions.

The crucial observation here is that, contrary to common belief, *the primary contributors to the economic or political system failures are*, not primarily the ill-willed intellectually-adults around, but *those innocents* who did not have the chance or the motivation to develop themselves and *remained intellectually-children throughout their lives.*

The Responsibilities And Rights Of Individuals

THE RESPONSIBILITY OF THE INDIVIDUAL

As explained above, each individual plays the roles of both a consumer and a supplier of labour in the economy, and a voter in the political system. Thus, he interacts with the society, such that his behaviour in these roles effect the welfare of the society. It is, therefore, his responsibility and duty to become an intellectually-adult and reach an adequate level of social awareness to contribute to the welfare of the society.

Reciprocally, it is each individual's right to demand all the other members of the society to become intellectually-adults, as their choices will effect the welfare of the individual as well. Therefore, *it can not be the personal freedom of any member of the society to remain to be intellectually-childish.*

DEMANDING FREEDOM TO CHOOSE WITHOUT HAVING ABILITY TO CHOOSE

Historically societies have done their best to get and keep their right to choose, politically and economically, and they naively believed that such right is equivalent to the freedom to choose. Unfortunately, *the right to choose has no practical meaning unless it is accompanied with the ability to choose the rational option for oneself* among the many.

Having the ability to choose requires becoming an intellectually-adult. However, *while societies demand the freedom to choose, they fail to demand the opportunity to develop their ability to choose*. For this reason, many decisions they have made and are still making among the choices they are given, were not and are not to their own best interest.

Even worse, their lack of intellect makes them fail to demand to be presented all the available choices – while somehow it so happens that the missing choices almost always contain the best ones for the individual and the society.

THE UNRECOGNIZED RIGHT

As the world is getting ever more complex every passing day, it is getting harder for each individual to make rational decisions (as a consumer and as a voter) that will enable the society to have well functioning economic and political systems.

It therefore becomes the basic right of each individual to demand a heavy investment in increasing the Social Intellect of both oneself and all the others in the society. Unfortunately, the demand of societies for this basic right has been almost non-existent throughout history. And, as resources are always limited, when the society does not demand something, it does not get it. And it is paying a higher and higher price for the lack of such demand every passing day, without being aware of it.

1.3 Why Is The Society Losing Social Intellect?

Social Intellect Is A Relative Concept

Social Intellect is a relative concept in two separate dimensions. One dimension concerns the intellectual level of a society with respect to those of the other societies, the superiority of which will bring comparative advantage in both economics and politics. The other dimension, the one that is more important in the search for the optimal allocation of resources to maximise the welfare of the society, is *the intellectual level of the society compared to the complexity of the economic and political environment in which it needs to survive.* And that is where even the economically advanced societies started to fall behind and experience severe troubles within the latest decades.

It is crucial for a society to realize that when a society is not adequate in the second dimension, even if it has comparative superiority in the first one, that will not be enough to save its own economic and political systems in the long run.

A MATTER OF RELATIVE INTELLECT

Advanced societies used to fool themselves on the assumption that their intellectual level is rising as their education systems are getting better and spreading wider. To start with, the effectiveness of current education systems in increasing Social Intellect is very questionable. For the sake of the current discussion, however, assume that they are really increasing the absolute level of Social Intellect of the society. Still, *if the complexity in the economic and political environment is rising faster than the increase in the intellectual level of the society, then the Social Intellect of the society is actually falling in relative terms.* In other words, the more complex the world becomes, the relatively less intellectual the society gets, although in absolute terms its current members may actually be much better educated than those in the past generations. And when the relative Social Intellect of the society falls, economic and political systems based on the assumption that the society remains intelligent enough, will not be working properly anymore.

Therefore, societies that used to be intellectually advanced in the past are becoming or will become intellectually inadequate unless they can increase their average intellectual level and social awareness in pace with the increasing complexity of the world. And the complexity of the world is increasing at a never-before-seen pace, almost exponentially.

How Has The Society Been Rising Its Social Intellect In The Past ?

In the older decades mutual interaction among societies were limited. Electronic communication was under-developed with respect to our day and social media networks were non-existent. Globalisation was not wide spread. Labour mobility was minimal. All in all, developments used to stay local and spread only slowly in an attenuated manner, if they spread at all. So societies were almost isolated from each other, life was relatively simpler, and changes were slow and limited in nature. Under those conditions where the complexity of the world was rising slowly, learning through daily exposure to social developments and experience gained through trial and error might have been sufficient to develop social awareness to an adequate level. In those days, getting older meant getting wiser.

But as will be discussed in detail next, in the integrated world of our day, each society is immediately and strongly effected by any development in any part of the rest of the world. This creates a pace of change that has not been experienced before, and now attaining social awareness through the natural ways of the old days is not practically possible anymore. Just on the contrary, if an individual can not keep up with the developments around him, he may actually get more and more intellectually-childish as he gets older.

Why Is The Relative Social Intellect Of The Society Falling ?

In the latest decades, the rise of globalisation resulted in the mutual integration of the economies of many societies, although the societies are minimally aware of it. The spread of electronic communication and the increase in labour mobility introduced a further dimension of integration in cultural aspects and thus inevitably in politics, while the societies are totally unaware of it. *These developments caused a sudden and significant increase in the complexity of the world, and therefore a sudden and significant loss of Social Intellect in all societies,* at a time when they were unprepared to deal with it. Now the societies are strongly and immediately effected by almost any development at anywhere else in the world, totally out of their control, and they do not know how to handle such complexity.

OPTIMAL ALLOCATION OF RESOURCES ?!

As explained in the previous sections, the Western Social Order, based on Free Market Economy and Democracy, assumes that individuals will act rationally, and by doing so, they will enable the optimal allocation of the society's resources such that the society's welfare will be maximised. And acting rationally requires understanding causations, namely the chain of events from the reason(s) to the result(s). And as the world becomes more and more complex, due to the many developments including but not limited to those mentioned before, understanding causations is becoming more and more of a challenge for each individual.

In a world where there are many mutual interactions among societies and many other emerging complications (like technological developments or ageing of societies), the causation-relations are getting exponentially complex. First of all, now there are too many variables effecting any outcome. And worse, the relations of the outcome to most of the variables are non-linear, meaning that how a change in a certain variable effects the outcome also depends on the changes on other variables, making understanding of their relation and thus forecasting the potential outcome of any action extremely difficult.

These create a terribly difficult world for the societies to understand. On the one hand, as the world is changing fast and a lot, and that is effecting every society, *the optimal allocation of resources for each society must be changing over time*. On the other hand, the complex nature of the new world makes it *extremely difficult to understand how the optimal allocation must change*.

A CLOSER LOOK AT THE DYNAMICS OF CHANGE

Developments occur all the time, but with different emergence speeds and magnitudes. Some developments are so significant that they require a major search for a new optimal allocation of resources. Some of these occur suddenly, but most develop slowly without being noticed for a long time, and then getting realized suddenly, cause an economic or social shake up at the time of their realization.

Any major development causes a permanent change in the way the society works, which in turn requires a change in the optimal allocation of resources. For instance, introducing automation to the production lines in factories will cause higher unemployment, which in turn necessitates more socially inclined changes in certain policies (thus, requires a change in allocation of resources) to take care of the now unemployed members of the society.

If each major development occurred after the necessary changes in the optimal allocation of resources for the previous development have been identified and applied, life would have been much easier for the society. Unfortunately, major developments usually come one after the other, without letting the society adjust itself to those that came before them. In such cases, their effects overlap and make life so complicated that the relative Social Intellect of the society falls way below the level required for the proper functioning of the economic and political systems. And that is exactly what has been happening lately.

THE MAJOR DEVELOPMENTS OF THE RECENT PAST

Many of the major developments in the latest decades actually originated from two main sources.

The first is technological advancements, where,

- development of new sectors based on information processing and communication technologies decreased the demand for capital and unqualified labour, thus created growth but increased inequality,
- the winner-takes-it-all nature of network economies brought monopolization and vaporised competition,

- increased automation in production increased efficiency and growth, but decreased the demand for unqualified labour, and thus increased unemployment and inequality,
- advancements in medical sciences lengthened life spans beyond expectations and undermined all existing social security systems based on the short-life-span forecasts of the past.

The second is globalization, where

- free flow of goods and services resulted in trade imbalances between societies and transferred wealth from one to the other, while within many societies fruits of resulting economic growth was not shared fairly and thus increased inequality,
- free flow of labour resulted in both immigration and the moving of production facilities to other societies, and resulted in an increase in profitability of the global corporations due to utilizing cheap labour, but increased inequality at home,
- free flow of capital through the global banking and credit systems enabled a flow from societies with trade surpluses to those with deficits, hiding rising inequality behind the debt-financed consumption in the receiving end,
- corporate activities with a global span merged many markets into one single global market and created global monopolies with excessive profits, but decreased competition at the expense of both the consumers and the labour.

Each society is supposed to handle all these developments simultaneously, while even one of these is significant enough to create a shake up in the economic and political systems. To make matters worse, the simultaneous occurrence of these developments amplify each others' effects, as it happened in decreased competition and increased inequality. These two troublesome end-results will be discussed in detail in Books Two and Three of this series.

When many major developments come in one after the other in such a fast sequence, adjustment of the optimal allocation of resources becomes a continuous process, never stabilising. To survive through this new ever-changing complex environment, the society will need to have a higher Social Intellect than ever before. Or, it will need to have extreme luck. For the time being societies are praying for the second – and doing nothing about the first.

The Downward Spiral

The hidden danger with losing Social Intellect is that, the more the individual or the society lose Social Intellect, the less they are aware of it, and therefore the less they try to improve it, and thus losing Social Intellect becomes a self-feeding downward spiral. As will be discussed in the coming books of this series, once Social Intellect starts to weaken, cheating spreads in the economy and competition decreases, inequality rises, the middle class weakens, cheating spreads further into politics, democracy weakens, then concentration of power emerges and dominates both economics and politics, and finally the society loses democracy to some form of hidden-autocracy to drive the final nail on the coffin of its social order.

Chapter 2 : WHAT HAPPENS WHEN SOCIAL INTELLECT WEAKENS

Social Intellect is not a luxury, but a necessity for the proper functioning of the western social order based on Free Market Economy and Democracy. Reading backwards, if and when Social Intellect weakens, structural failures and other major undesirable consequences will emerge.

The structural failures have to be discussed separately for Free Market Economy and Democracy, and that will be done in Chapters 3 and 4, so they are just briefly touched below. However, some major undesirable consequences are common to both economics and politics, and they will be discussed for both in Sections 2.2, 2.3 and 2.4.

2.1 Structural Failures

WHEN THEORY MET PRACTISE

The magic mix of Free Market Economy and Democracy (with all their local variations) seemed to be the perfect sustainable solution for a civilized social order, with the inherent checks and balances between economics and politics. All that was required of the society, were simply the *flawless awareness* of and the *perfect reaction* to these systems' dynamics.

Unfortunately, societies are made up of people who are both unaware and incapable of executing their duty of behaving as defined and expected in theory.

Naturally, problems arose when theory met practise.

NOT THAT WE WEREN'T WARNED

Economic and political systems are developed by philosophers, economists, statesman and many individuals in many societies over centuries. Each system, including the latest magic mix, is based on certain *preconditions* and *critical assumptions.* These preconditions and assumptions have to be fulfilled completely, or at least adequately, for the proper functioning of these systems. There are also *inherent weaknesses* in the structure of these systems that can not be completely eliminated, thus in practical application they have to be minimised, through different means to be determined under case specific conditions, such that they will not jeopardize the proper functioning of these systems. Most developers of the economic and political systems were already aware of these shortcomings in practise, and have already warned societies to try to handle them properly while applying these systems.

A NOT-SO-BRIGHT APPLICATION

Over the latest decades, societies forgot about or neglected these preconditions and assumptions, and defied the principles. They have completely forgotten, or deliberately made to forget, that the inherent weaknesses have to be taken care of somehow. Thus, even in the economically advanced western countries, the eventual systems that the societies ended up with, which were believed to reflect variations of the magic mix, actually had not much in common with the ideal definitions, nor had been cured for their already well known weaknesses in practise. Naturally, they failed.

AND A NOT-SO-BRIGHT CONCLUSION

And the societies managed to follow their not-so-bright application, with an equivalent not-so-bright conclusion. They have started to think that something was very wrong with the social order based on Free Market Economy and Democracy, *based on their experience on the misapplication of these systems.* The latest but the clearest sign of losing Social Intellect.

THE ONLY CHOICE

The seemingly perfect economic and political systems of the western world have spectacularly failed in 2008. There is nothing better to replace them. From an economic perspective, the carrot and the stick, namely the reward versus the punishment dynamic, is vital for economic progress, as excessively socialist systems do not work in the long run. From a political perspective, freedoms and rights, and the control of the governing authority by the society through a democratic system, can not be replaced by autocratic or populist systems. The only real choice is to analyse what were missing or have gone wrong, and more importantly, to understand and admit why all those have happened. Then the core cause of the system failure can be cured before the economic and political systems collapse irrevocably.

2.2   The Spread Of Cheating

Competition And Allocation Of Resources

Economics theory states that, in a free (and therefore competitive) market, supply and demand meet and balance out each other, to reveal the so-called equilibrium market price for a good or service. Guided by this price mechanism, the market participants on both the supply and the demand sides can determine how they should allocate their resources in the most appropriate manner. The maximisation of the welfare of the society requires this *optimal allocation of resources,* and that in turn *requires adherence to the principles of competition by all participants.*

Principles Of Competition

The main principles of competition that are necessary to keep the welfare of the society at a satisfactory level are briefly explained next. There is another principle required to maximise the society's welfare, namely the *equality of opportunity in preparing for the competition.* However, that will be discussed in Book Two of this series, as for the scope of this book it will suffice to consider the ones below. Please note that, these principles are initially explained through an economic viewpoint below, but they are completely valid from the viewpoint of politics as well, as will be explained immediately afterwards.

NO BARRIERS TO ENTRY OR EXIT

In theory, when there are no barriers to entry or exit, any potential competitor willing to participate in the market should be able to join the competition, and any existing competitor willing to leave the market should be able to do so. In practise, however, there will always be some barriers based on either the nature of the market or the regulations governing that market. As long as such barriers are kept at a rational level, meaning that they are not unnecessarily strong or prohibitive, they will not prevent a healthy competition. Reading backwards, anyone (individual or corporation) willing to decrease competition for his own benefit and at the expense of all other competitors and the society, will try to rise barriers for others once he is in the market.

NO CONCENTRATION OF POWER

The second principle of competition is that there should be no concentration of economic power within any market. In practise, this means that no single competitor or a group of competitors should be able to determine or even effect the price formation in the market. Therefore, let alone the extreme cases of monopolies or oligopolies, any over-concentration that effects the price formation in a market will harm the optimal allocation of resources. For this reason, some variation of anti-trust regulation is developed in almost all advanced economies.

ALL COMPETITORS PLAY BY THE SAME RULES

The third principle states that all competitors at all times should be competing under the same rules and regulations, meaning that no competitor should be able to violate or even bend the prevailing rules at any time.

SOCIETY'S INTERESTS SHOULD BE PROTECTED

The fourth principle, which is the least known and unfortunately the least applied in practise, is that there must be proper regulation to ensure that the rules of competition in the market are set and enforced to protect and promote the long-term interests of the society, beyond balancing the interests of those who participate in the market as producers on the supply side and as consumers on the demand side[3]. And naturally this principle is the most vulnerable for cheating purposes, especially against the society.

Who Sets The Rules Of The Game

As all the principles mentioned above require some degree of regulation, it should be clear that competition can only survive in well regulated markets. In other words, how well the competition works will primarily depend on how good the rules and regulations are set. Regulation, however, is a product of the political system. Therefore, *the maximisation of the welfare of a society, which initially seems to depend solely on the well functioning of the economic system, actually requires the well functioning of the political system as well.* And exactly for that reason, anybody who would want to decrease competition for his own benefit will at some point target the regulatory bodies - and that practically means everybody in the political system from top to bottom.

REGULATORY FAILURE

A regulatory failure is the case where the regulator willingly or unwillingly serves the interests of some concentrated interest group at the expense of the society, either through mis-regulation, or a lack of necessary regulation, or its failure in enforcing the existing regulation.

Among the variations of regulatory failure mentioned above, lack of regulation is the best known one, probably because such missing regulation stemming from the over advertisement of freedom during the latest decades, became too widespread with too strong negative consequences that could not go unnoticed even in societies with weak intellectual development. However, the other two variations that are much less noticed also have equally significant negative consequences. The market may be so mis-regulated that even when all the competitors obey all the regulations, the society can still get harmed, or worse, the mis-regulation may create an unfair advantage to the benefit of a certain competitor against its rivals. And finally, the regulations may not be enforced completely, especially on some competitors in the market, such that while other competitors have no choice but to obey them, these competitors do not, and thus force their rivals out of competition, at the expense of the society.

The role of the regulator in the economy, as the rule maker for the best interest of the society, is indispensable. And exactly for that reason the society has control over the regulator through the political system in democracies, in theory. In practise, however, whether the society can utilise that control to maximise its own interests or not, depends primarily on the intellectual level of the society.

What Is Cheating ?

In a Free Market Economy, the primary principle has to be first maximising the value created for the society in line with the principles of competition, and then, getting one's fair share of the value created. This is the rational and ethical but the difficult way to create value for oneself and for the society simultaneously. Naturally, many people prefer a much easier and faster way, namely cheating. *Cheating, therefore, is simply defying the principles of competition.* In other words, cheating is to promote one's own interests at the expense of those of the society, by acting against the principles mentioned above. And in practise, different ways of cheating are limited only by one's imagination.

Consequences Of Cheating

When all the competitors on the supply side stick to the principles of competition, all will be competing fairly with the others, as result of which the value created for the consumers on the demand side will be maximised, and the rest of the society will at least not get harmed and at best be better off. However, when some of the competitors start to cheat, like erecting barriers or bending the rules, they will gain an unfair advantage against their rivals. Utilizing this unfair advantage, they will start to eliminate their rivals and create a *concentration of power* in the market, which in turn *decreases competition*. And decreasing competition will translate into higher prices and/or worse products for the customers. And finally the Cheaters may try to further increase their benefits through preferring certain profit maximising behaviour even though it has definite negative side effects on the rest of the society.

Competition (And Cheating) Does Not Only Cover Economics

Although we have first discussed the concepts of competition and cheating from an economic perspective, all these   principles of competition and the related arguments are completely valid for competition in politics too. Just keep in mind that, in politics the competitors on the supply side are the politicians, the consumers on the demand side are the voters, and the rest of the society are the young generation who can not vote yet, but whose future is shaped by the current political decisions and the actions of the current voters and politicians.

In politics, on the supply side, politicians offer their services covering legislation and execution, to the voters on the demand side. When all the politicians stick to the principles of competition, the value created for the voters will be maximised. However, when some of the politicians start to cheat, they will gain an unfair advantage and will start to eliminate their rivals to create a concentration of political power, which in turn decreases competition in politics. And decreasing competition will then translate into worse services (inferior legislation and execution) for the voters. And finally the Cheaters may try to increase their benefits further through preferring certain benefit maximising behaviour even though it will have negative side effects in the long run on the current young generation.

Wrapping Up Some Pieces

It should now be clear that in both economics and politics, defying the principles of competition, namely cheating, results in a misallocation of resources, which in turn decreases the overall welfare of the society.

The fact that there is an overall decrease in the welfare of the society in case of cheating, reveals a significant conclusion: while on the one hand, the benefit of the Cheaters will increase, on the other hand, the benefit of the rest of the society will fall much more than the benefit of the Cheaters. In other words, the Cheaters will get a relatively smaller benefit in return for a very high expense for the rest of the society, as the total welfare of the Cheaters plus the rest of the society will fall due to cheating[4]. This extremely significant conclusion will be discussed in detail in Book Two of the series.

For the time being, it will suffice to remember that adherence to the principles of competition can very effectively be ensured through making and enforcing proper regulation, and regulation is a product of the political system. Also remember that, when the Social Intellect of the society weakens relative to the complexity of the world, it can not make rational decisions, including political ones. Therefore, regarding economics, the society can not properly react to cheating *through the political system*, and regarding politics, it can not properly react against cheating *within the political system*.

Therefore, *when Social Intellect weakens, the society can not protect itself against cheating in either economics or politics, and then cheating spreads and spreads, and eventually harms the welfare of the society to the point where the stability of both the economic and political systems fall in danger.*

In both economics and politics, the freedom to choose becomes meaningless unless the individual has the ability to choose rationally. And exactly for that reason the Cheaters of all sorts and sizes defend the society's freedom to choose in their relevant fields, but never promote the development of the society's ability to choose. And this observation alone should be enough to see what the society should do to protect its own interests.

What Should The Society Do To Minimise Cheating ?

As will be discussed in Chapters 3 and 4, even if there were no cheating, weakening of Social Intellect ruins the economic and political systems in many other ways. However, cheating pours fuel to the fire.

FEEDING GROUNDS OF THE CHEATERS

As discussed previously, in every society there are intellectually-children and intellectually-adults, with all the shades in between. And an intellectually-adult may act ethically or cheat shamelessly, again with all the shades in between. And as discussed before, the Cheaters feed on the intellectually-children. Therefore *the higher the ratio of intellectually-children in the society the more and the faster cheating can spread* and ruin the society.

In nature, if you want to annihilate certain species, one way is to destroy them directly, but another more effective way is to destroy their feeding grounds. In a similar fashion, if the society wants to get rid of the

Cheaters, a direct way is to have better regulation and better enforcement, but another (preferably additional) way is to wipe-out their feeding grounds, namely, to educate the intellectually-children and increase their Social Intellect and awareness.

An additional trouble here is that, in the recent decades, as the world is getting more and more complex ever faster than before, even some of the individuals who were once intellectually-adults are starting to fall back to becoming intellectually-children. Therefore, *as the pace of increase in complexity can not be slowed down in any society, the intellectual advancement of the society must speed up*. And that can only happen if the society heavily invests in social education, in terms of time, effort and resources. And although this is far from being easy or trivial to accomplish, it is not impossible anymore, as will be discussed in later chapters.

2.3   The Rise Of Intellectual Inequality And The Leading Elite

Dimensions Of Inequality

Inequality comes in many dimensions.

Economic inequality is the income or wealth inequality between the individuals within a society. In theory, an excessive rise in economic inequality will result in a political demand to change economic policies, and therefore it can be cured through democratic means.

Intellectual inequality is the inequality of Social Intellect between the individuals within a society. While the Social Intellect of the society is weakening as explained before, only a minority within the society manages to keep or rise their Social Intellect, and the majority simply loses theirs. This in turn drives intellectual inequality to higher levels than ever before. In the economic and political systems, such excessive levels of intellectual inequality results in the population-wise domination of the society by the intellectually-children, who are destined to fall prey to the Cheaters among the intellectually-adults, and that in turn will ruin the welfare of the society in the long run. In the decades in the distant past, it used to be possible to cure intellectual inequality naturally as the individuals slowly accumulate social experience throughout their lives. However, in the complex and continuously changing world of our day, a much faster sort of social education is necessary to develop Social Intellect and awareness. Unfortunately, the lack of Social Intellect also means the lack of demand for curing it, so weakening Social Intellect is becoming a time bomb within our economic and political systems.

Professional inequality is the inequality in having some professional expertise versus having none, usually referred as being qualified labour versus unqualified labour, with all the shades of grey in between. Having professional expertise means a lot when an individual enters the labour market as a supplier and will most probably place him on the winning side of the economic inequality, and vice versa.

Consequences of Rising Inequalities

THE ANIMAL SPIRITS WITHIN

The main characteristic that differentiates humans from the rest of the species inhabiting our world is not our biological code, but the intelligence gap between us and them. Although other species have sorts of their own intelligence as well, we consider this intelligence gap between us and the others to be excessive, such that it gives us the moral right, supported by our superior might, to harm those other species as we see fit. At our current level of civilization, our animal spirits deny us any moral obligation towards the other species, and we feel no guilt in neglecting or even harming them.

If this self-assigned moral right of the superior to dominate the inferior, based on the difference in levels of intelligence, has stayed only between humans and other species, it would not have been within the scope of this book. However, our animal spirits are a part of our genetic code, and we consciously or unconsciously maintain the same logic when it comes to the relations among the individuals within a society. In an historical context, it is difficult to deny that, *individuals, when they perceive a huge intelligence gap between themselves and the others, neglect any norms of civilized action, and animal spirits dominate their behaviour against the others*.

The increase in all types of inequalities between the individuals, at a never-before-seen speed, tends to worsen the relations among the individuals within the society every passing day. From an economic perspective, further advances in automation, artificial intelligence and efficiency in general, will sooner or later make some individuals within the society simply unnecessary and expendable. From a social security perspective, those individuals on the winning side of the inequalities, under the influence of their animal spirits, will feel little responsibility to help the ones on the losing side. And the ones on the losing side will not like the idea of being at the mercy of the winners through whatever means anyway. All together, rising inequalities will invite a loss of social peace, eventually resulting in economic and political system failures. Therefore, it may be a good idea for the society to focus on preventing excessive inequalities between the individuals, before it is too late to solve the problem peacefully.

START WITH INTELLECTUAL INEQUALITY

A major problem with these inequalities is that, each inequality feeds on the others, and therefore the chicken and egg problem grows exponentially when left to its own devices.

Any macro-economic problem, including excessive economic inequality, has to be cured through a political demand for an economic policy change, but unless the Social Intellect of a society is adequate, the political system will not work properly to serve the interest of the society.

Any demand to decrease professional inequality, which has to be primarily based on equality of opportunity, also requires a political demand, and again will fail as long as the Social Intellect of the society is not adequate enough to make the political system function properly.

To cut the long story short, the problem of rising intellectual inequality has to be cured first, to ignite the political demand to cure the rest. Unfortunately, the weakening of the Social Intellect of the societies is rising intellectual inequality even further, and thus feeding the trouble in the others as well.

The Society And The Elites

In line with the classification of inequalities above, it is possible to differentiate the groups of elites within a society, as the Economic Elite, the Intellectual Elite and the Professional Elite. There is no theoretical definition of being an elite in either dimension, but for practical purposes the term elite refers to those who excel to the highest ranks (say to top 1-3%) in each dimension.

The Intellectual Elite are those with the highest Social Intellect, who can see the forest without getting lost among the trees. *Every society needs its Intellectual Elite, as they will be guiding the society in the right direction in this ever-changing complex world of our day.* Therefore, any society that lacks the Intellectual Elite, or can not appreciate who they are, or does not value their guidance, or lose trust in them (for the right or wrong reasons), is destined to get lost in the forest.

The Economic Elite are those with the highest level of income or wealth within the society. As will be discussed in Book Two of this series, economic success can come through many ways: merit, luck, excessive risk taking or cheating. In many cases, it is difficult to diagnose from outside which of those is the main reason behind economic success, and in many cases, not one but a blend of these is the answer. However, it is clear that Social Intellect is not a prerequisite for economic success.

And the Professional Elite are those with the highest level of expertise and competence in their respective fields. However, Social Intellect is not a prerequisite for professional success either.

It directly follows that, if the society mistakes the Economic or Professional Elite for the Intellectual Elite, and ends up following their guidance instead of that of the Intellectual Elite, that journey rarely ends well. Unfortunately, that is what usually happens when Social Intellect weakens.

THE INTERCONNECTION OF THE ELITES IN THE SOCIETY

Once we define the elites as those who excel to the highest ranks in their relevant dimensions, it becomes clear that most people in the society do not belong to any of these elite groups, simply because those who are by definition way-above-the-average can not be in large numbers, as otherwise they would have been the average themselves. And within the small number of members of a society who belong to some elite group, some may belong to just one group of elites, while some others may belong to two or even three groups simultaneously.

The figure below shows all the possible combinations among the elites in the society. Intersections of elite groups in the figure shows those who belong to more than one group. For instance, IP shows those who are both Intellectual and Professional Elites, while IPE shows those who are in all the three groups simultaneously, etc. Notice that, while being an Economic or Professional Elite does not necessarily make one an

Intellectual Elite, it does not necessarily exclude him from the ranks of the Intellectual Elite either. They are just independent dimensions.

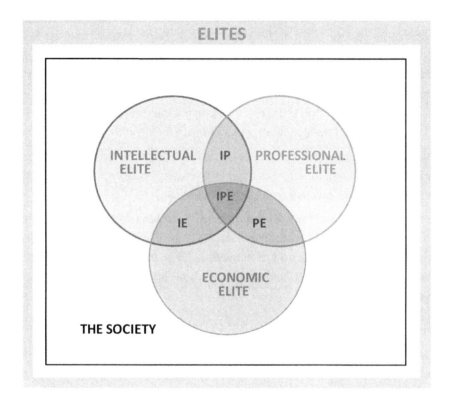

In an intellectually-adult society, all these combinations can and probably will exist, and the intersections among the elites will be frequent. However, finding such a society is not an easy task, even if there is one hiding somewhere. The practical cases are rather different, and we will utilize this simple figure to conceptually illustrate some common patterns.

The Economically Advanced Politically Lost Society

In the latest decades, the exponential advancements of two sectors, finance and high tech, have created a new major group of people who are both Professional and Economic Elites in many societies, led by the United States. This is actually a sign that brainpower is replacing capital as the major, or at least an equally important, source of personal economic advancement, which should be taken as a very welcome development in the economic functioning of those societies. However, the excessive hard work required to follow such paths to success may have left no time and effort for the development of Social Intellect for those people, and the situation depicted in the figure below may have emerged.

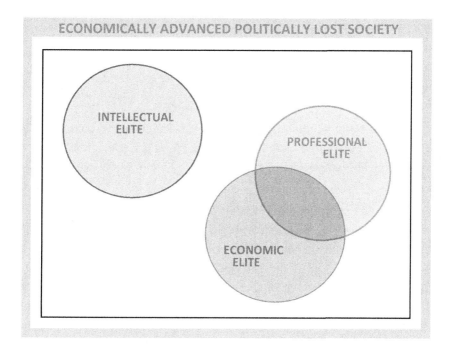

This would have been no problem if these societies could have analysed this situation properly and followed the guidance of their Intellectual Elite in making their economic and political decisions. Unfortunately, in these societies it is believed that if someone has a bit of intelligence and ability, he will use it to promote his own well being, as absolute self interest is the undisputed logical path in the prevailing economic theory, and therefore, the Economic Elite by definition are considered to be the most intelligent members of the society. And worse, anybody who has not attained an Economic Elite status, by this definition, must not have outstanding intelligence, and therefore also lacks the intelligence required to become an Intellectual Elite. When taken together, these will naturally create the impression that the Intellectual Elite can only be among the Economic Elite, and nowhere else. This line of thinking promotes the Economic Elite to the Intellectual Elite status whom the society should follow, even though in reality their Social Intellect may be very limited. And when the society choses the wrong elite to follow, it will get lost in its economic and political choices, and sooner or later end up in a system failure.

The Cheater-Dominated Society

A CLOSER LOOK AT THE ECONOMIC ELITE

In line with the previous analysis in Section 2.2, two sub-groups of the Economic Elite can be defined : the Fair Playing Economic Elite (who sticks with the principles of competition) and the Cheating Economic Elite.

While the Cheating Economic Elite is the most harmful for the welfare of the society, the Fair Playing Economic Elite are vital for the survival and the economic development of the society. Therefore, in order to survive and prosper, the society must maximise the number of the Fair Players and minimise the number of Cheaters. However, doing so requires the ability to distinguish between the Cheaters and the Fair Players, and that is not easy especially when the Social Intellect of the society is inadequate. And knowing that, the Cheaters do their best to hide behind the Fair Players and make themselves indistinguishable.

And a catastrophic combination emerges when the Social Intellect of the society weakens, such that, on the one hand the society starts to be guided by the Economic Elite, while on the other hand, the Economic Elite is dominated by the Cheaters.

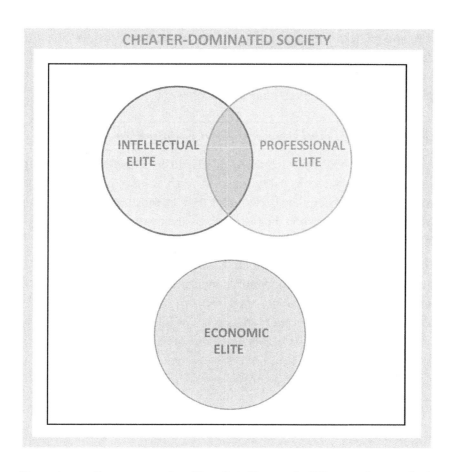

To make matters worse, the Cheating Economic Elite mostly use their wealth to access political power. They may do this directly through lobbying on politicians and bureaucrats, or by offering them current or future benefits, or indirectly through guiding the intellectually-children in the society to support policies that benefit the Cheaters. In any case, in such a society, becoming an Economic Elite will not require to be a professional, let alone being an intellectual, but rather, cheating becomes the norm for attaining and keeping an Economic Elite status. Consequently, the Economic Elite do not intersect with the other two groups, and the situation depicted in the figure above arises.

Thinking backwards, if we face a society where the Economic Elite do not intersect much with the other two groups, although in theory this may just be a coincidence, in practise it gives us reason to suspect that the Economic Elite may be heavily dominated by the Cheaters, which in turn will mean that the Social Intellect of the society is inadequate to run a social order based on Free Market Economy and Democracy.

Social Intellect And Deciding The Leading Elite

Every society needs its own Intellectual Elite to guide it through the macro developments it faces every passing day in the complex global environment. Consequently, the better their Intellectual Elite, the better will be their guidance, and the faster will be the increase in the welfare of the society.

Having a reliable Intellectual Elite, however, is just the beginning. An additional but equally important condition is the adequacy of the intellectual level of the society, as it is the society who decides whom to follow. If the Social Intellect of the society weakens, even if the society happens to have the best Intellectual Elite somehow, it will not be able to appreciate and follow them, but rather be guided by a wrong elite and eventually face the negative consequences discussed before.

2.4 Misjudgement Of Social Values And Contributions

A Matter Of Want Versus Demand

The words want and demand are usually used interchangeably. In economics and politics, however, their difference is of crucial importance. Want is the simple wish to have something. It has no significance. Demand is to be willing and able to pay for something you wish to have. It is all that counts. The concept of payment in this context is not limited to monetary / economic terms, but also includes spending time and effort for the realization of an issue, or changing economic or political choices in reaction to the non-existence of an issue.

To illustrate, consider the toys-for-big-boys, like luxury cars, yachts, planes etc. Their suppliers do not care who wants them, as almost everybody does. What counts is whether anybody demands them, namely whether there is somebody who can and will pay for them. Plain want of the crowds is of no use, apart from increasing the motivation of those who can pay for them. But if there is nobody who can pay for them, such motivation has no use either. In that case, nobody will supply these toys, even if they can.

The case for the toys-for-big-boys does not have much of an importance from a social viewpoint. However, the difference between want and demand is crucial in other basic aspects of social life, naturally including economics and politics. Put simply, if the society does not demand free markets, fair competition, social security, democracy, liberty, human rights and all similar social values, it simply will not get them, or will lose them in case it somehow happened to have them.

Trouble With The Macro Demand For Social Values

NO FREE RIDING ON HEROES

Throughout history, rather than demanding the social values mentioned above, societies looked for heroes to struggle for and earn those values on behalf of the society. In economic logic, this corresponds to societies' free riding on the personal sacrifices of those heroes to attain such social values. Now may be a good time to realize that such free rides do not exist anymore as the stock of heroes has depleted long ago. Therefore, *societies must learn to demand whatever social values they are willing to have or to keep*.

Many values societies have today, attained as a result of such free rides in the past, are not even well appreciated, and even worse, are usually taken for granted by the current generations, under the fatally false assumption that there is no chance of losing them. It is time for societies to realize that no social value is granted to any society forever, and if the society fails to appreciate them before losing them, it will just lose them first, appreciate them next, and will have to demand them back again by paying a much higher price later.

To put in a clearer context, *in all economic and political matters, the society needs to decide and keep in mind at all times how much it appreciates and therefore demands certain social values*. And, it has to remember that *it will continuously be tested to reveal its preferences*, such that any social value that the society fails to appreciate and demand accordingly, will be taken from it by some Cheaters who will benefit from the non-existence of that social value.

Many examples easily come to mind. If the society fails to appreciate the value of free markets, too much state intervention may benefit some minority groups with good political ties, at the expense of the society. If the society fails to appreciate the value of fair competition, creation of barriers to entry may result in a concentration of power in the market that will decrease competition and will harm the customers or even the rest of the society. If the society fails to appreciate the value of social security, a decrease in tax burden and a fall in redistribution may fail to cure excessive inequality. If the society fails to appreciate the value of democracy, it may have to live with autocracy. If the society fails to appreciate the value of liberty, it may lose some basic freedoms based on excuses like promoting security or national interests. If the society fails to appreciate the value of human rights and treats the immigrants or members of other societies inappropriately, it will face social stress within the society in the long-term. The list may go on forever, but the message is clear: *if the society does not demand to keep or promote some social values, sooner or later it will lose them.*

DEMAND ARISES FROM INTELLECT

At the heart of the problem lies the fact that the intellectually-children can not differentiate want from demand. To start with, they do not demand to be socially educated and properly informed on major economic and political issues, so they remain innocent for a lifetime, never demanding anything ever again.

And if the society is dominated by the intellectually-children, then it fails to demand anything for its own interest, but just keeps wanting them, and naturally gets nothing in return. The Cheaters, however, strongly demand things to their own interest, at the expense of the society, and get most of them, in both economics and politics. And in time, as the harm done to the society eventually accumulates to unbearable levels, a system failure will follow.

As the society starts to lose Social Intellect, it will either react in time to cure it before its too late, or will just end up becoming an intellectually-children dominated society. And then it will be just a matter of time before the society loses the social values that ensure both the sustainable increase of its welfare and the stability of its social order.

Trouble With The Micro Demand For Individual Contributions

In the basic economic logic, individuals should be rewarded in line with their contribution to the welfare of the society. The concept of contribution here covers both economic and all other sorts of social contributions. And the reward can either be in terms of some monetary value, or in terms of other social values like recognition or respect, or some combination of all.

The obvious trouble here is in determining the value of an individual's contribution to the society. In principle, the demand vs supply relation in the market determines the value of an individual's contribution and rewards the individual accordingly. In this approach, the individual creates a net benefit to the society that is equal to the value of his contribution minus his reward. Sounds like a simple solid logic.

The implicit assumption behind this approach is that the society is able to value the contribution of the individual properly and fairly. And this is where the logic usually blows up.

For everything to work properly, the society should be able to value the contribution of the individual rationally, and should determine and limit its reward to the individual such that the resulting net benefit to the society will be positive. And if the individual is also rational, he will expect to be rewarded fairly, such that he will not engage in a process where he is rewarded too little relative to the value of his contribution.

If and when both sides act rationally, a sustainable fair balance between the individual's contribution to the society and his reward will be attained naturally. The trouble starts when the society is unable to value the contribution of the individual rationally.

In some cases, the society may overpay to the individual with respect to his contribution, such that the resulting net benefit to the society will become negative. This will result in a waste of resources on activities that only bring a marginal value, if at all, to the society.

In other cases, the society may underpay to the individual, as a result of which the individual will have to give up his potential engagement in some activity that would create significant value to the society. This will mean a shortage of resources at where they are most needed.

In both cases the society misallocates its resources including its human capital. As we have already discussed, such misallocation will eventually cause a significant decrease in the welfare of the society. In both cases, therefore, the society's lack of ability to value various contributions properly will cost heavily to the society in the long run – if not in the short one.

The trouble gets worse in intellectually-childish societies, as the situation is exactly like children valuing candies more than medicine. It is important to understand that, when the individual producing candies gets overpaid while the individual developing medicine is underpaid, the problem lies with the society. It is not the fault of the medicine-developer to be less valued, and it is not the fault of the candy-producer to be more valued either. Under such circumstances, many bright individuals will naturally align their supply with the demand of the society to be rewarded adequately, and there will be much more candies and much less medicine produced in that society. In line with the dynamics of demand and supply, the society eventually gets what it wants -and what it deserves-, but of course, any society that misaligns its demands with its long-term benefits will definitely suffer the consequences. At best, it will develop way slower than its maximum-attainable-development-speed, if it develops at all. At worst, it will lose the stability of its social order and fall into chaos.

The ability of the society to value contributions rationally depends on its intellectual level. If the intellectual level is low (or weakens significantly), more short-term and pleasure oriented contributions will be overvalued, while contributions that will create significant value for the society in the long-term, but will mostly require short-term sacrifices, or just lack the short-term charm, will be undervalued or will not be appreciated at all. And a high price will be paid for that in the long run.

If the Social Intellect of the society has already fallen, the only solution is rising it to the level where the society can make rational valuations and properly align rewards with contributions to maximise its long-term welfare. But, as discussed before, in the complex environment of our time, it is not possible to achieve such a rise in the Social Intellect when its development is left to its own devices. And worse, as the weakening of Social Intellect also prevents the appreciation of the situation by the society, the necessary demand for a cure may not arise at all.

As discussed before, in social matters everything starts with politics. In the case of significantly losing Social Intellect, therefore, the only hope of the now- intellectually-childish society is to be lucky enough to somehow be governed by politicians with enough goodwill to act as statesman - practically meaning heroes. These heroes, on the one hand, will take the necessary steps to increase the Social Intellect of the society, while on the other hand, make a proper resource allocation to keep the welfare of the society and the stability of the social order intact until the society becomes an intellectually-adult one again. And they will act in that manner although they are aware of the fact that such heroic moves will shorten their political career, as children get angry with elders who replace candies with medicine. After all, self-sacrifice is an expected attribute of a hero.

Unfortunately, having the luck to somehow being governed by heroes coming out of thin air does not sound like a very probable story. Therefore, it may be much better and safer for the society to try not to lose Social Intellect to start with.

Chapter 3 : CONSEQUENCES OF LOSING SOCIAL INTELLECT IN A FREE MARKET ECONOMY

3.1   Self Interest And The Invisible Hand

THE MYSTERIOUS INVISIBLE HAND

The idea of the existence of an invisible hand was initially introduced in the 18th century by Adam Smith, who believed that free competition in the market creates an optimal allocation of resources, such that when each participant in a market tries to maximise his own interests, the interest of the society is also maximised. This process of automatic maximisation of the interest of the society out of the maximisation of individual interests is conceptually presented as the existence of an invisible hand that carries out this function.

The idea of an invisible hand sounds attractive, as once an individual believes in its existence, all that he needs to do is just acting selfish without any need to worry about anybody else, since the invisible hand is there to protect and promote the best interest of the others. Furthermore, by promoting his own interest, and by the help of the invisible hand, the individual actually serves to the best interest of the society, so he deserves to get spiritual satisfaction out of his honourable behaviour, rather than feeling guilty of being selfish.

Ever since its introduction, the idea of the invisible hand had, and still has, many advocates in many societies, some of whom sincerely believe that an invisible hand with this perfect ability really exists, while others simply think that it creates a very convenient excuse to cheat on the society.

Thanks to its strong attraction and widespread acceptance, the idea of the invisible hand, and the permission for selfishness that is offers, got heavily integrated to both the economic and political systems of many societies.

THAT RATIONAL SELFISH INDIVIDUAL

The combined system of Free Market Economy and Democracy defines a rational individual as one who acts to maximize his individual self-interest, without any need to worry about what happens to the society. This freedom is granted by the invisible hand, which makes sure that everything the individual does in his own personal interest will eventually benefit the society.

By promoting the idea of the invisible hand in the Free Market Economy, the society creates selfish individuals who are expected and approved to act only in their self interest. Coincidentally, Democracy further supports the legitimacy of selfishness. In a one-person-one-vote system, each individual has a vote of his own, thus has the right to pursue and protect his self interest, without any need to think of the others, as the others will also vote thinking of their own interests, and some invisible hand will maximise the interest of the society somehow.

People can go to the extremes once they are freed of the responsibility of the consequences of their actions. Therefore, when individuals are set free to maximise their own interest without any need to think of their consequences for the society, there is no limit to the harm they can inflict on the society.

Fortunately, most people behave rather contradictory to the interpretations of rationality within the invisible hand framework most of the times, as they behave ethically and with social responsibility. That may either be because they are not aware of the freedom-to-act-selfish granted to them by the invisible hand, or because they suspect that the invisible hand may not be working as effectively as advertised, so that it is for everybody's best interest to act in a socially responsible manner.

WHY THE INVISIBLE HAND FAILS

The main message of the invisible hand, that selfish behaviour is not contradictory to rationality or ethics, but just on the contrary is required by them, does great harm to the society whenever the invisible hand fails to function. And it fails a lot.

Some reasons of its failure are well illustrated in game theory - a discipline of thought that has major implications for economics and politics.

One such reason is that, even when the outcome of a game (an economic or political formation) makes all the participants happy, it may still harm the society at large, if it has negative consequences that effect some third parties within the society who were not participants in the game. The invisible hand can not take care of such harm to non-participants of a game in the absence of proper regulation to protect the interests of the society, and thus becomes rather ineffective in creating an optimal outcome for the society out of the selfish decisions of the participants in such cases. And for that reason, any Cheater who wants to serve his own interests at the expense of the society, is a firm advocate of free-markets-without-regulation in which the invisible hand should reign without intervention.

A second reason is the existence of some specific cases that can in general be represented in some form of *prisoners' dilemma* in the jargon of game theory. In such cases, the rational decisions on an individual basis, left to be aggregated by the invisible hand, eventually serve neither the interests of the individual nor the interests of the society. Such strange but common cases, with significant implications in both economics and politics, will be discussed in detail in later sections.

And the third reason is the simplest but the strongest of all.

LACK OF SOCIAL INTELLECT & THE MISERY OF THE INVISIBLE HAND

The main argument behind the invisible hand is that, it maximises the interest of the society, provided that all the individuals maximise their own interests. Implicit in this argument is the critical assumption that each individual will be able to maximise his own interest to start with. For that assumption to hold, each member of the society has to be an intellectually-adult. Only under that condition the invisible hand can have a chance, at least in some cases, to function.

While most discussions focus on whether the invisible hand exists or not, few notice the fact that, if the individuals frequently fail to make rational decisions, as it happens when their Social Intellect is inadequate, then, even if there is an invisible hand, it is destined to fail miserably. As the famous saying goes, the invisible hand can not be expected to create long-term wisdom for the society out of the collective short-term foolishness of the individuals.

The intellectually-children, therefore, as they fail to pursue their own interests, not only harm themselves, but also harm the society, as the invisible hand can do nothing else but accumulate the individual mistakes to eventually create a system failure.

LIVING WITH THE INVISIBLE HAND

There are many cases where the invisible hand can not be left alone to optimise the interest of the society, in which, rather than giving an overdose of freedom, the society needs to set the rules of the game properly to protect its own interests. Nevertheless, the invisible hand exists in a conceptual sense, and although it is neither theoretically nor practically perfect, it still serves a vital function as long as free competition is desired in both economics and politics. Therefore, it is in the best interest of the society to maximise the performance of the invisible hand. And the higher the Social Intellect of the society, the better each member of the society will promote his own interest within the prevailing boundaries of freedom, and therefore, the better the invisible hand functions.

Reading backwards, if the society starts losing Social Intellect, the functionality of the invisible hand deteriorates and its harm may eventually dominate its benefits, paving the way for a system breakdown in both economics and politics.

3.2   Asymmetry Of Information

The Bull Story Versus The Full Story

Anyone who has been to Spain to watch a bull fight is probably told the story of the bulls. The bulls that fight in the arena against the matadors are not regular bulls that one can meet elsewhere, as regular bulls most of the times choose not to fight with the matador when taken to an arena. And when there is no fight, there are no spectators, and then there is no bull fighting business left. Thus, the so-called fighter-bulls are bred under specific conditions and prepared for the fight through certain procedures, so that they will be angry and fierce when taken to the arena, and will always choose to fight.

This bull story, told to everyone who is interested, is a true story. But it is not the full story. How many people would notice that they were not told what happens when and if a regular bull is chosen for a fight, and, just as may happen on a few occasions, the bull actually chooses to fight?

The critical trick in breeding the fighter-bulls is that, a fighter-bull never sees any man standing on his feet or walking, until it is taken to an arena. What it only sees until the fight are men-on-horses, and therefore it only gets familiar with a non-existing creature with four-legs-and-two-heads. When it is taken to an arena, it initially faces such non-existing but familiar creatures, to which it attacks and mostly causes severe damage (practically to the horses only, not to the riders), while itself is also being heavily wounded by them. At the final stage, for the first time in its life, it faces the matador, a man on his feet, waving a flag near his body. The fighter-bull, which has no memory of such a creature from the past, probably assumes that the floating flag is a live creature and attacks to it – as the matador stands still. It repeats its desperate attempts to kill that floating creature many times, during which it gets further and fatally injured by the matador each time it passes by. All this happens within twenty minutes, at the end of which the bull meets its inevitable destiny.

The critical trick in the fight is that, it should not go on for long, simply because if the bull has enough time to learn, through experience gained after repeated attacks to the flag, that it should actually attack the standing creature, the matador will have a slim chance of surviving the fight against the speed and strength of the bull.

Going back to the question above, if a regular bull which has previously seen and therefore has learned to recognize a human being standing or walking, is taken to the arena, and if the bull chooses to fight, it naturally attacks to the matador directly -rather than bothering with the floating flag- and the fight does not last very long, resulting in the wrong ending. Murder is not fun to watch when the victim is the human being.

When one is told that regular bulls do not attack most of the times, and that creates a problem in bull fighting business, that information is true. However, the real problem is what happens when the regular bulls choose to attack, and that part of the story is conveniently forgotten to be told. The story on fighting-bulls, which is the only part that is told, is true but not complete. The fighting-bulls are not only specifically prepared to fight, but actually prepared to lose the fight. Thus, the fight in the arena is not a fair fight between a man and a bull (in which the man would have a very slim chance to survive), but rather, it is a terribly unfair fight between an expert man and an ignorant / naive bull, that is manipulated from the start to result in the desired ending. And, chances are that, learning the full story behind the true story will change one's opinion on bull fights. Admiration for the matador will fall, pity for the bull will rise, and that will not be good for the bullfighting business.

Though the story of the bulls is a sad one, it would not be within the scope of this book if it were not an illustration of what is happening to whole societies in real life, in both economics and politics.

Creating Market Failures

Asymmetry of information refers to the case where the participants on the supply and demand sides have different levels of information on the issues relevant to a transaction. The idea that such asymmetry can cause market failures or even total destruction of markets, was introduced by George Akerlof in 1970s[5] and later brought him a Nobel prize.

To illustrate the basic concept from an economics perspective, assume that in a particular market 8 different qualities of a product are supplied, with 8 different values ranging from $10, $20, $30 ... up to $80. And assume that there is perfect asymmetry of information such that the consumers can not differentiate between the qualities of those products until they buy and use them. Under those assumptions, what is the price a consumer should be willing to pay to buy for one of these products?

Because of the incapability of the consumers to differentiate between the various qualities of that product when making a purchasing decision, all producers will initially argue that their product is worth $80. And there may even be some consumers buying that product at that price initially. However, through trial and error the consumers will soon realize that there are actually 8 different qualities of that product, and they may hit any one of them randomly. Therefore, they will now be willing to pay the price of only $45 to that product, as that is the average value -also called the expected value in the economics jargon- that they will get through a random selection. But when the price falls to $45, all the producers whose products are worth more than $45 will leave the market. Therefore, continuing the trial and error process, the consumers will soon realize that they now face products with values ranging between $10 and $40 randomly, so they have to adjust the price to reflect the new average value they will randomly hit in the market, namely to $25. But when the price falls to $25, all the producers whose products are worth more than $25 will leave the market too. Therefore, the consumers will soon realize that they now face products with values ranging between $10 and $20 only, so now they have to pay $15 for the random product. And this price will drive out the producer whose product is worth $20 out the market too, leaving only the worst product with the value $10 in the market. And as soon as the consumers realize this, they will decrease the price to $10 and the market will reach its final equilibrium.

Therefore, because of the information asymmetry, only the worst quality (lowest value) product will remain in the market, and only for that product a fair market, where the price reflects the value, will be established. All the other 7 varieties of products with higher qualities will have to leave the market as they can not get the fair price for the value of their product. If there were no information asymmetry, however, there would have been 8 separate markets with 8 different prices, all of which reflecting the fair prices for the respective qualities of the respective products. The existence of the information asymmetry, therefore, has not only destroyed the markets for the other 7 products, but also permitted the survival of only the market for the product with the lowest value for the consumer. Considering the different qualities of this product as vital parts of the whole market for this product, the information asymmetry has resulted in a market failure.

A CLOSER LOOK

The dynamic presented above is an illustration of a complete destruction of a market because of an excessive asymmetry of information, but such extreme cases are rare. However, the existence of a moderate asymmetry of information is such a common case in real life economics and politics that there may only be a few exceptions, if any.

To see what happens when partial information asymmetry exists, consider a market where there seems to be perfect competition between the suppliers (no barriers, no price setting power etc.), however, the consumers can only appreciate the differences in some attributes of the product but are unable to observe the differences in some other attributes, as it happens with most of the products of our time. In such cases, the perfect competition naturally works only on the attributes of the product that are observable by the customer. There can not be, and therefore there is not, any competition on the attributes that the consumer is not aware of or can not observe. As the information asymmetry is only partial, the market failure is also partial and thus is more difficult to observe.

To illustrate, assume that the consumer can observe the colour and size of a product, but not the chemicals or materials it is made of. Then, as competition gets fierce, some of the producers will start to use the cheapest quality chemicals with the lowest cost -even though these chemicals may somehow harm the consumer in the long run- to be able to decrease prices and gain competitive edge while still staying profitable. Once this dynamic starts, the rest of the producers face two options. They may reject to use those harmful materials and as a result can not decrease their prices, and become uncompetitive, and leave the market.

Or, if they want to survive in the market, they will have to start to utilize the same materials to be able to decrease their costs and therefore their prices to competitive levels. Therefore, once a competitor starts to use the advantage of the asymmetry of information to its own benefit at the expense of the society, all others have to follow suit in order to stay competitive. In our case, all the surviving producers end up using those low-quality cheap chemicals in their products.

Notice that, as there is still perfect competition over the product, based on the attributes observed by the consumers, the decrease in production costs will sooner or later be reflected in the overall price of that product, and the eventual profit margins of the producers will not change much. However, the consumers are permanently stuck with the worst quality materials used in the unobserved attributes of the products. The bottom line is that, *even in competitive markets, any attribute of any product that goes unobserved by the consumers will be subject to the dynamics of information asymmetry and end up at the lowest quality possible.*

As the dynamics of markets cover all sorts of relations between counter parties in economics and politics, the negative implications of this simple conclusion are paramount on the welfare of the societies.

Asymmetry Of Information Is An Inherent Weakness

In principle, the maximisation of the welfare of the society through competition requires all relevant and correct information to be available to all participants in every market. Unfortunately, this is almost never the case in practise, and *asymmetries of information exist as an integral part of any market where supply meets demand for any product or service, in both economics and politics. This makes asymmetry of information an inherent weakness of both the economic and political systems.*

In the simpler environments of the good old days in the distant past, the information asymmetries between the participants in any market used to be much less than they are today, keeping the negative effects of the partial market failures limited on the society. But in today's environment which gets ever more complex every passing day, individuals need to make a million decisions on a million complex issues continuously, from economics to politics, and in aggregate they need a huge amount of information to make rational decisions on every issue. Unfortunately, the Social Intellect of the society can not keep up with this rising complexity. Most members of the society are incapable of processing that much information even if they were presented the full stories on every issue. They naturally consent to making decisions based on inadequate information presented to them in economic and political matters, and do not demand more. Consequently they are exposed to ever decreasing percentages of the full stories, increasing the information asymmetries ever further. As the society's Social Intellect weakens further, information asymmetries skyrocket and the negative consequences of all sorts of market failures they cause may eventually accumulate to reach unacceptable levels for the society. And that paves the way for potential system failures in the long run.

Perception Management

Our previous discussion regarding market failure reveals that, a supplier will not invest in improving an attribute of a product unless the consumers have the ability to appreciate the increase in its value that such improvement will bring.

Any improvement will require either research or production expenses, or both, that will eventually increase the production cost and therefore the price of the product, while increasing its value. Therefore, any improvement that will increase the price of the product while the increase in its value will not be appreciated by the customer, will actually decrease the demand for the product. Therefore, for the supplier, the lack of awareness of the customers on an attribute is a practical obstacle for any improvement on that attribute, as investing in improving it will not bring any competitive advantage. And this simple observation has many practical consequences.

If a supplier believes that he can have some improvement on an attribute that will rise the product's value, while that specific attribute is not noticed by the customers, it makes sense for the supplier to start a marketing campaign to draw attention to that attribute so that the improvement will increase his competitive advantage, and if the campaign succeeds, both the producer and the consumers will benefit from it. This approach is both rational and ethical.

But what if the attribute that the supplier can improve to distinguish his product is not critical enough to increase its value? Then perception management comes to the rescue. To increase his competitive advantage, the supplier now has to deliberately create a misperception through a marketing campaign, arguing that the attribute that he managed to improve is actually a very critical one for the value of the product but was just failed to be recognized by the customers. If the campaign succeeds, it creates a different sort of asymmetry of information, where, that particular attribute which the supplier knows to be unimportant, is promoted to be an important one in the eyes of the consumers, guiding them to think that the promoter's product is better than those of his rivals. As the demand shifts to that product for no real reason apart from the creation of a misperception, it will actually cause a misallocation of resources within the economy, harming both the consumers and the society.

Just as perception management can be used to over-promote a positive attribute of one's own product, it can also be used to over-promote a negative attribute of a competitor's product. To illustrate, a food producer may correctly announce that the ingredient X used by his rivals doubles the probability of developing some sort of illness in consumers, but just fails to mention that the probability of getting that sort of illness is 1-in-a-million for an individual, and by consuming that ingredient X, it doubles to 2-in-a-million, a totally neglectable change in comparison to all other much more important issues that can create health problems.

In general, *perception management is based on presenting correct but misguiding information*. In that regard it is not illegal, or even not completely unethical as there are no lies involved, and is therefore a perfect tool to misguide the society in economic and political issues.

WE ARE NOT ALONE, UNFORTUNATELY

Every individual makes very many choices every day, but they don't do it alone. Many individuals, especially the intellectually-children, try to free ride on others' decisions and choices, the phenomenon known as the tendency to follow the crowd. This presents a perfect opportunity to those who try to misguide the society through perception management. Once they start to change the behaviour of some people, many others who try to free ride on the choices of those people will follow suit. This will amplify the credibility of the misperception and create a snowball effect. Perception management is a more effective and more dangerous tool than generally assumed, and its danger is amplified when the Social Intellect of the society weakens and the intellectually-children start to dominate the society.

A Tool For The Cheaters

As discussed above, asymmetries of information exist as an integral part of any market, in both economics and politics. This inevitable existence of asymmetry of information gives a powerful tool to those who want to cheat on their rivals or on their consumers or on the society.

Cheating utilising asymmetries of information can work in different ways. In the simplest case, the Cheaters deliberately present only some portion of the whole story, such that it is true but will most probably be misunderstood by the society, especially by an intellectually-childish one, and result in their acting in the benefit of the Cheaters rather than of their own. It is important to notice that Cheaters prefer to present partial but misleading truths to false information, as the latter is easier to detect and to reject, while incomplete truth can be as misleading as direct lies, but more effective as it can not be proven to be false.

As in the bull fight, the trick with any interaction involving two sides with interests contradicting each other in economics and politics is that, the side with the full or superior initial information will try to achieve its desired outcome before the other side accumulates enough experience and develops a counter strategy to protect its own interests. The strategy of the Cheaters is, therefore, to act fast to set the stage through supplying the partial but misleading truth, and benefit from this environment as much as possible until the society accumulates enough experience and wakes up to reality. And the more the Social Intellect of the society weakens, the easier the stage can be set and the longer the game can be played by the Cheaters.

The Need For The Experts And The Regulators

THE CURSE OF HAVING A WIDE RANGE OF PRODUCTS

Societies are generally happy with having a wide range of different and non-competing products, and it is easy to understand this attitude as having many options to choose from never hurts in principle. However, the situation may actually be somewhat more complicated.

As new products are developed continuously, and a million different products are offered to the consumers, the consumers will start to have less and less time to examine each type of product in detail, meaning covering all attributes, before making a final decision. Therefore, in all products, the information asymmetry between the producers and the consumers will naturally increase.

To illustrate, when there were only a few types of non-competing products (say only ovens and refrigerators), the consumers could examine four or five attributes regarding the competing products in each product type. But when there are many types of non-competing products (say ovens, refrigerators, dish washing machines, mixers, microwaves) the consumers will have less time to learn about each type and thus will only examine one or two outstanding attributes on each. Therefore, unnoticed attributes for each type of product will increase, and through the chain of events explained previously in this section, the consumer will eventually face lower quality or even partially harmful products in all markets without even knowing it. And if the prices decrease, as it usually happens due to decreasing costs based on lower quality materials used in the unnoticed attributes, *the consumers will believe they have benefitted out of the competition, while actually they are paying less primarily because they are purchasing much inferior products.*

Therefore, as more and more new products are offered to the consumers, the information asymmetry between the producers and the consumers in every product significantly increases. As the number new products arriving to the market everyday is increasing exponentially, the society needs to develop means to handle these ever increasing information asymmetries.

FREE RIDING ON OTHER CONSUMERS

Naturally, not all consumers are equally informed on all attributes of any product. If most customers of a product are aware of the most outstanding attributes of a product, then as the competition among suppliers will span all those attributes, the final product will be of high quality and available at a fair price with respect to its value. If this is the case, any individual with little awareness on that product may just free ride on the awareness of the rest of the customers, and can share and enjoy the high quality and fair priced outcome.

This opportunity to free ride on others is available, by definition, if and only if most consumers of a product have high awareness. But in practise, this comes out to be a very weak assumption. Just on the contrary, most consumers are little aware of the relevant attributes, while they assume that somehow many other consumers are there to make a fair judgement and keep the producers competitive on every attribute. This naive but widely shared assumption on the availability of a free ride on other consumers with high awareness is a phenomenon commonly seen in intellectually-childish societies. On the contrary, intellectually-adult societies realize that they simply can not free ride on each other, but just need to create other means to take care of such information asymmetries.

RELYING ON EXPERTS ?

In today's environment where too many different products exist, and a fully informed wide customer base is absent for any product, one obvious solution comes out to be relying on expert opinion in making choices. However, deciding who is an expert on a particular issue, or on a product in our case, is not an easy job for the society. Moreover, the goodwill of the experts has to be somehow checked as well, as knowing the truth does not necessitate sharing it with the society, but just on the contrary the expert may have some other incentive to keep it a secret. There is no rule saying that experts can not collaborate with the Cheaters.

Therefore, whenever the consumer can identify an expert and become sure of his goodwill, he can free ride on the opinion of that expert on a particular market, but unfortunately, when there are so many different products, identifying the experts with goodwill for each product is a difficult task.

NEED FOR A REGULATOR

This brings us to the conclusion that, the consumers not only need expert opinion, but also need to have some way of systematically finding reliable experts (in terms of both ability and goodwill) for each and every major product. As that systematic search for each product can not be achieved on an individual basis, the economic and political system had to be designed to provide that function, namely, to provide regulation whenever there are potential information asymmetries between the producers and the consumers.

The initial role of the regulator is to try to minimize information asymmetries by making the suppliers reveal vital information regarding all the attributes of their products to the consumers, enabling the customers to make rational choices. And when this is practically not possible, like in the cases where some attribute is too technical to be understood by the consumers, or requires too much time and effort to be properly evaluated, the next role of the regulator is to ensure through proper regulation that the interests of the consumers are well protected.

When the asymmetry of information is significant between the supply and the demand sides (which happens to be the case in practise in most markets when left to their own devices) and a regulator does not exist or is not functioning properly, then, as explained above, competition brings out the worst possible outcome for the consumers. It is therefore important to keep in mind that, *as there is no way of escaping information asymmetries in any market, the existence of regulators is not a matter of choice of economic policy, but is a necessity for the proper functioning of any market.* And once again, regulation is a product of the political system, and the political system can work properly if and only if the society has adequate Social Intellect. Reading backwards, the weaker the Social Intellect of the society gets, the weaker will be the political system and the resulting regulation, and the stronger will be the damage on the economy caused by the information asymmetries in the markets.

From Micro To Macro

The cases examined in illustrating market failures, perception management and the curse of having a wide range of products are all taken from micro-economics, based on the behaviour of the individuals within the scope of the markets. As can be easily guessed, *asymmetry of information also influences the understanding -or misunderstanding- of macro-economic policies and therefore the shaping of the political choices of individuals and societies.* It should not be difficult to guess that, the weaker the Social Intellect of the society gets, the higher will be the information asymmetries and the worse will be the functioning of the economic and political systems. We will discuss these in the next chapter.

3.3 Agency Problems

Ability And Willingness

At some distant past in history, upon receiving my MBA from the Wharton School, I have joined a major Bank in New York, and to my pleasure, was immediately placed in an upper-management training program. One day during the program, the instructor was discussing how to use the balance sheets, income statements and cash flows of a company to analyse its financial ability to pay back its debt to the bank, which I already knew in all imaginable detail. While I was busy with admiring my span of expertise on the subject in silence, suddenly, theory met reality. "It is crucial that a company has the ability to pay back its debt" the instructor said, "but what really counts is whether it will be willing to pay it back."

At that point, the concept of the willingness of the counter party to behave in the way it is supposed to behave has permanently integrated itself to my line of thinking and became a basic component of all my analysis on economic and political issues ever after. Fortunately, it is easy to analyse the willingness of the counter party if you can read minds. The trouble starts if you cannot.

The Agency Relation

Everyday, individuals have to deal with a large number of issues, and on each they have to make an analysis to be followed by a decision and an action. Depending on their interests and expertise, they may handle some of these personally, but for most others they need to utilise agents who will act on their behalf. This practical necessity creates principal - agent relations in very many issues, spanning economic and political matters as well.

The first recognized and best known type of agency relation is the one between the shareholders and the managers of a company, and that is why the concept was initially born and developed in the field of corporate finance. In principle, the shareholders, namely the principals, expect the managers, namely the agents, to act in the shareholders' best interest in making decisions regarding the business of the company. However, in light of costly previous experiences of others, the shareholders have reasons to suspect that the relation may not be working in exactly that way in practise.

The principal - agent relation exists in many fields in economics and politics. On a micro-economic scale, in almost any market, there is an asymmetry of information, usually coupled with an asymmetry of expertise, to the disadvantage of both the consumers and the society. In such cases, the consumers and the society, as principals, are delegating the duty of analysing the market and making and enforcing the appropriate regulations considering the best interest of the consumer and the society, to the regulator, as their agent. In a similar fashion, on a macro-economic and political scale, when the society, as the principal, elects a politician to a legislative or executive duty, it expects the politician, as its agent, to behave in the best interest of the society and maximise its welfare.

THE TROUBLE WITH THE AGENCY RELATION

When a principal delegates the duty of acting on his behalf to an agent, one primary assumption behind that delegation is that the ability of the agent in dealing with that specific issue is much superior than that of the principal. And few mistakes are made in practise in that dimension, especially if the principal is an intellectually-adult one. But a second primary assumption, which is even more significant, but much weaker, and therefore in which the practical problems mostly arise, is that the agent has the perfect goodwill to act on the best interest of the principal independent of the agent's own interest. Unfortunately, most of the times the best interest of the agent is not the same as the best interest of the principal, and this *conflict of interests* may change the behaviour of the agent, such that the agent acts to promote its own interest at the expense of that of the principal, and creates an *agency problem*.

By the nature of the principal - agent relation, there is not only an asymmetry of expertise, but also an asymmetry of information, both to the advantage of the agent, between the agent and the principal. These twin asymmetries give birth to and amplify agency problems in practise.

THE TROUBLE WITH LOSING RELATIVE INTELLECT

As the complexity of the world rises, the relative intellect of most individuals fall on most issues, including those subject to principal - agent relations. However, in an agency relation, relative intellect does not weaken equally on both sides. As the agent has more expertise due to his concentrated interest on the issue subject to the agency relation, and more motivated to keep up with and analyse the recent developments and their effects regarding that particular issue, the agent's relative intellect falls much less than that of the principal. Reading backwards, *as the complexity of the issue subject to the agency relation rises in time, the principal's relative intellect falls much more than the agent's,* as the asymmetries in both the information and the expertise on that particular issue rise to the disadvantage of the principal. In a micro-basis, therefore, rising complexity, and thus falling relative intellect, pours fuel to the fire in agency problems.

The significance of this observation is not limited to micro-economic relations, but unfortunately it has severe consequences on both the macro-economic and political matters as well, as will be discussed in Chapter 4. For now, it will suffice to underline that on a macro basis *weakening Social Intellect worsens the agency problems where the principal is the society.*

The Trouble With The Agents

On the agent's side, the agency problem arises simply because the agent may be inclined to cheat on the principal, especially when the principal is considered to be too naïve to be aware of such cheating. The agent therefore serves its own interests at the expense of those of the principal's whenever there is a conflict of interest.

To complicate matters, by mere chance, the interest of the agent may sometimes be in line with that of the principal, at which the agent will naturally be acting at the best interest of the principal as well, making it more difficult for the principal to detect any cheating that may occur on other occasions.

As discussed above, when the complexity of the world rises, both the asymmetry of expertise and the asymmetry of information between the agent and the principal also rises, to the disadvantage of the principal. This will significantly decrease the ability of the principal to detect any cheating on the agent's side. As a consequence, the amount of cheating the agent may get away with -without being detected by the principal- increases, which in turn increases the potential benefits the agent can get for himself at the expense of the principal. And this naturally motivates the cheater to cheat further on the principal.

This dynamic may be a clue on why troubles are rising on macro-economic and political fronts as the world gets more complex and the Social Intellect of the society weakens.

CONCENTRATED BENEFITS DISTRIBUTED COSTS

As will be discussed in detail in Book Two of this series, during the last couple of decades, in very many major markets, competition is decreasing and the producers on the supply side are getting more and more concentrated, while the number of consumers on the demand side are increasing to reach millions for each product. This practically means that, any changes in regulations that may slightly tilt the market to the benefit of the producers at the expense of the consumers, will significantly rise the revenues of each producer, while the rise in costs per customer will probably be infinitesimal. Therefore, the producers have a very strong incentive to lobby on the agents of the society, namely the regulators and legislators, to misguide or persuade them through any means to act in manners that are not at the best interest of the society. The principals, namely the consumers and the society, however, can not respond in kind for two reasons. First, the society totally fails to see the causality relation between decreasing competition in individual markets and the cumulative decrease in its overall welfare. Second, the attention of each individual to any single market is very limited as a result of being a customer in very many different markets simultaneously, thus, he barely realizes the change against his interests in any particular market. Therefore, the consumers, and thus the society, usually fail to detect the ever rising agency problems in the economy.

The Trouble With The Principals

There is no escape from asymmetries of information and expertise in any agency relation, and therefore, the principal in the agency relation must devise ways to deal with the agency problems. One common way to handle the agency problem is to align the interests of the principal and the agent such that there will be minimal conflicts of interest to cheat on. An additional approach is to evaluate the performance of the agent properly such that the agent can be rewarded fairly in case of success and will be punished in case of failure. When these two are achieved, the agent's motivation to cheat will be minimal. Unfortunately, on the principal's side, the agency problem survives simply because the principal fails spectacularly in handling the problem through either of these ways. And as the relative intellect of the principal weakens, his ability to handle agency problems deteriorates further, skyrocketing agency problems and their harm to the principal and the society.

FAILURE TO ALIGN INTERESTS

In any agency relation, the simplest way to decrease conflicts of interest is to create an incentive system such that the agent wins when the principal wins, and the agent loses when the principal loses, both in *fair proportions*.

Although establishing a fair compensation system sounds simple and straightforward, most principals fail to accomplish it, mostly deliberately, as compensating the agent fairly when the principal wins creates an additional explicit cost to the principal that decreases his net benefit. Instead, most principals prefer to minimise such explicit compensation, and in turn face a much higher cost implicitly, and thus end up with much less of a net benefit eventually as the agent cheats to promote his own interest at the expense of that of the principal.

To make matters worse, in such cases, from the agent's viewpoint, prioritizing his own interest against that of the principal sounds more like a self-defence against the unfair treatment of the principal, rather than unethical cheating. The principal's deliberate unfairness, which actually stems from the inadequacy of his Social Intellect, actually gives the agent a great moral excuse to protect his own interests and not considering such action as cheating.

It is true that by promoting his own interest the agent is behaving unethically, however, it is also true that, by not compensating the agent fairly, the principal himself is virtually creating a significant conflict of interest. In other words, the principal expects the agent to behave ethically, although himself acts unfairly and therefore unethically, when he rejects to share the benefits of success appropriately. The critical mistake here is that, on the surface most principals do share some of the success with their agents, however, instead of a fair win-win situation, they try to impose an I-win-a-lot-you-win-a-little approach. This creates some sort of hidden conflict of interest, and although the principals prefer to keep a closed eye on it, the agents never fail to notice.

FAILURE TO ASSESS PERFORMANCE

Even if a principal sets a fair compensation system to minimise the conflicts of interest between himself and the agent, that will not solve the agency problem unless the principal can fairly evaluate the performance of the agent and compensate him accordingly.

The difficulty of assessing the performance of an agent comes from the fact that, the eventual outcome, called the absolute performance of an agent in the jargon, is a combined result of two sub-components. One is the external conditions under which the agent has performed, which were totally beyond the control of the agent. The other is the inherent value of the agent's decisions, called relative performance in the jargon, which are under the direct control of the agent. *For proper assessment of the agent, the eventual outcome has to be evaluated relative to the external conditions prevailing at that time, in the sense that the principal must evaluate what-has-been-achieved versus what-could-have-been-achieved.* In other words, the assessment of the agent must be based only on the inherent value of its decisions, namely on his relative performance.

Sometimes the external conditions are stable and have negligible effect on eventual outcomes. But at other times, there can be pretty strong headwinds or tailwinds whose effect may dominate the eventual outcome. The principal needs to be aware that, when there are strong headwinds (negative external conditions), the eventual outcome may be negative even if the decisions of the agent are correct. Similarly, when there are strong tailwinds (positive external conditions), the eventual outcome may be positive even if the decisions of the agent are wrong. And as external conditions change randomly, the absolute outcomes dominated by their effect can not be any indicator of the future performance of the agent, so no assessment can be based on them. On the contrary, the relative performance of an agent, as it is under total control of the agent, is the only reliable indicator of his future performance, and therefore must be the base of a rational and fair assessment.

If the agent knows that he will be rewarded when his decisions add value to the principal, and more importantly, he will not be punished for external negative conditions beyond his control, his loyalty to the principal, meaning his goodwill, will naturally be much higher. But when the opposite is the case, namely when the fate of the agent depends on conditions beyond his control, his future with that principal will definitely be limited, and therefore his loyalty to the principal, and thus his goodwill, will be much lower. This is because of the simple fact that, the relative performance of the agent is within his own control, and provided that he has the required ability, is sustainable. The external conditions, however, are random, and therefore, sooner or later they will be negative. If the principal is assessing the agent on the basis of absolute outcomes, they will eventually part ways, and therefore, from the agent's viewpoint, keeping his goodwill will be an ethical but irrational approach. And *it is not wise for any principal to force his agent to make a choice between ethical and rational.*

THE TROUBLE WITH TIME HORIZONS

In both economics and politics, the time horizon in which individuals try to realize their goals is the key to most decisions, and this adds a further complication to the principal-agent relations.

The primary goal of both the individuals and the society is to maximise their welfare. The trouble here is that, what needs to be done to maximise welfare in the short-term mostly contradicts with what needs to be done for maximisation for the long-term, creating a crucial trade-off between sacrificing one for the other, such that striking an optimal balance between the short-term and the long-term is vital.

In many cases in agency relations, the principal himself is not sure which time horizon he prefers. In principle, most principals seem to prioritise their long-term interests. In practice, however, sacrificing short-term interests is not easily acceptable and may take actual priority. This dilemma on the principal's side leaves the agent at a position in which whatever he does may not satisfy the principal, and thus his future with the principal may be short in any case.

To complicate matters further, even in the cases where the principal sincerely demands an optimal balance between its long-term and the short-term interests, there may still be a time horizon mismatch problem, this time between the principal and the agent. This problem arises if the agent for some reason can not or does not expect to remain at the service of the principal in the long-term. When the time horizons of the principal and the agent are different, where the agent's horizon is naturally shorter, the agent may not target to maximise the long-term interests of the principal at all, but only focus on the short-term ones. Therefore, it is the principal's duty to make proper performance assessments periodically[6], to make sure that the agency relation will not fail at the expense of the long-term interests of the principal.

Although periodic assessments are a necessity, the situation will actually get worse if assessments can not be made properly. One such common case is when the principal fails to differentiate between the correct decisions made by the agent that necessitates deliberate sacrifices in the short-term for the sake of the long-term versus any wrong decisions. As discussed above, another common case is where the potential negative short-term effects of external conditions beyond the control of the agent are not taken into account and a negative outcome in the short-term is directly considered to be the agent's fault. The bottom line is that, in practice, the assessments made by the principal seals the agent's fate, and if these assessments can not be made properly, the agent's life will become a nightmare. In such cases, no incentive can persuade the agent to think for the long-term, and the principal actually seals his own unfortunate fate through his own failure in performance assessments. The only solution is to increase the intellectual level of the principal to enable him to make proper assessments, such that he can evaluate the long-term strategies pursued by the agent correctly and fairly.

WHEN RELATIVE INTELLECT WEAKENS

When the rising complexity of the world decreases the relative intellect of the principal on the particular issue subject to the agency relation, his risk of failure in aligning mutual interests and/or properly assessing the performance of the agent increases. This motivates or even forces the agent to take care of his own interest through other means, while the principal is becoming more defenceless against the cheating of the agent as the agent loses less of his relative intellect on that particular issue. Naturally, the agency problem worsens and both the principal and the society get significantly harmed – most of the times without being aware of it.

From Micro To Macro, Again

Needless to say, the failures of the principals on setting proper incentives for their agents and/or on assessing the performance of their agents are not confined to micro-economic issues. Just on the contrary, both the agency problems and their consequences exist on much larger proportions when the macro-economic and political systems of the societies are considered. These will be discussed in Chapter 4.

THE NEED FOR HONEST DIAGNOSIS

Principal - agent relations are widespread in macro-economics and politics. If a society, as the principal, insists on diagnosing any trouble within that relation as one solely arising from the agent's side, there is no way to cure it, simply because the trouble mainly lies on the principal's side. Therefore, *to minimize agency problems, both in macro-economics and politics, the society, as the principal, should rise its own Social Intellect first, and only then try to cure the agents' side.*

Chapter 4 : CONSEQUENCES OF LOSING SOCIAL INTELLECT IN A DEMOCRACY

4.1 Democracy And The Social Intellect Of The Society

In politics, it is said that each society is governed in the way it deserves. This is easy to understand in a democracy, as, by definition, the society decides who will govern them. It is also easy to understand that only an intellectually developed society can attain and sustain a functional democracy. And it is a well known fact that societies where the political system is based on some variation of democracy are better governed. However, the causation is usually misunderstood. *A society is not better governed because it is a democracy. A society is better governed only because it is intellectually developed.* Therefore, intellectual development of a society is the real cause behind both a better governance and a functional democracy, simultaneously. In this sense, good governance and democracy are just strongly correlated, but one does not necessarily bring the other.

In politics, the causation runs from the intellectual level of the society to its political system. Thus, the changes in the intellectual level of the society will determine the direction its political system will evolve towards.

DEVELOPING SOCIAL INTELLECT AND DEMOCRACY

In most cases of attaining democracy in history, societies slowly developed their wisdom by increasing their social experience and awareness through their own natural dynamics, thus intellectually grew up first, and then replaced autocracy with democracy.

Once a society develops its Social Intellect and attains democracy, as long as it remains to be intellectually-adult, it can stay as a functioning democracy, in a fortunate state of stable equilibrium. However, *contrary to what most societies believe, staying intellectually-adult is not easy and is neither granted nor comes for free.* And in today's world where the fast rising complexity of the environment is the norm, that belief can be the most fatal one for the future well-being of the society.

THE DANGER OF WEAKENING SOCIAL INTELLECT AND LOSING DEMOCRACY IN PRACTISE

Unfortunately, reaching the intellectual advancement level to deserve a democracy at some point in time, does not necessarily mean that the society will continue to deserve and thus remain to be a democracy.

Even if a society becomes intellectually-adult at one stage, there is no guarantee that it will stay so ever after. The world changes and societies integrate at a very fast pace, and thus staying aware of the latest technological advancements and the resulting social dynamics, including economic and political developments, requires continuous effort by the society to improve its Social Intellect line with all these rising complexities.

If the society fails to do so, in many cases due to *the laziness brought by the luxury of having achieved a satisfactory level of wealth and social security*, it may eventually fall back to being intellectually-childish again. Then, it will first face the risk of losing good governance, and eventually lose its functioning democracy to some sort of an autocracy. This time the autocracy will not be an explicit one, but most probably hide behind a fake democracy where the society's opinion is manipulated and the results desired by the Cheaters in both the economic and political arenas are obtained through a cover of democracy. But the cover can not hide the fact that the political system is not a functioning democracy anymore. And once the Social Intellect of the society weakens and some sort of autocrat-in-disguise comes to power, he will most probably be bright enough to take all the necessary precautions to keep the Social Intellect of the society as low as possible so that his political status will not be questioned or challenged. Under these conditions, the current autocrat may in time be replaced by another one, but the trouble with the political system will stay intact and the welfare of the society will hit the bottom. Unfortunately, *an autocracy within an intellectually-childish society creates another state of stable equilibrium* that may last for a long time.

THE INTELLECTUAL ELITE CAN NOT SAVE THE SOCIETY

The fairy tale, which very rarely comes true, is that each society can wait for a hero to save it and lead it to the heavens, practically meaning that the society is looking for a free ride on the ability, goodwill and the personal sacrifice of the hero. History shows that, in some rare cases when such a hero somehow happens to land on an autocratic political system as the autocrat himself, this may actually work out and the hero deliberately carries the society from autocracy to democracy.

Once a society becomes a democracy, however, there is no chance of other heroes to come around and save the society from falling back to autocracy-in-disguise. This is simply because, in democracies, the executive and legislative bodies are elected by the society, and the society generally appreciates, likes, trusts and thus elects those who are somewhat above the average intellectual level of the society, but not too much above that they look alien to the society. Therefore, it does not really matter how intellectual, wise, able, good willing and patriotic a potential leader may be, as he will still not be able to lead the society if the society is not intellectual enough to appreciate and elect him. What this means in practise is that, *it does not much help to the fate of the society even if it somehow produces some Extremely-Intellectual Elite, unless the society as a whole is intellectual enough to follow their lead.* Thus, *in a democracy, what determines the fate of a society is primarily the average Social Intellect of the society itself,* rather than the number of potential heroes it can produce.

Therefore, in a democracy, the fate of a society changes in line with the changes in its average intellectual level. And exactly for that reason, if there is a Cheating Elite, namely some combined team of economic monopolists plus a political autocrat-in-disguise, they will naturally do their best to prevent the intellectual level of the society to rise beyond its current low level. And this can be done in many ways, including mis-education starting from youth, mis-guidance by the help of bought out experts and incomplete flow of information ever after, and the distraction of society's attention to either surviving the day (for the economically worse off) or to irrelevant minor issues away from the real major deficiencies in the economic and political system (for the economically better off).

And to emphasize again and again, even if a society is intellectually-adult for the time being, unless it continues to develop its Social Intellect to cope with the developments around, it will fall back to becoming relatively childish in time, and the Cheaters with aspirations to create economic monopolies or political autocracies-in-disguise, will be more than happy to see and help that.

4.2 Should A Voter Care To Stay Aware?

When the social order of the society is questioned, politics is where it all begins. Politics decides the macro-economic policies. Politics drives the regulations on a micro-economic scale. Politics, through the legislative and executive bodies, designs and runs the social environment the individuals live in. Politics sets the inter-society relations from trade to war. To cut the long story short, politics sets the destiny of the society.

And in a democracy, the individual, as the voter, is at the heart of the political system. He indirectly controls everything, and therefore, his own destiny. Within that frame, the individual is expected to try hard to fulfil his role as a voter in the best possible manner, at least in principle. And that starts with getting adequate social education – the details of which will be discussed in Chapter 6. But unfortunately, it does not end there.

Even if an individual has adequate social education, it still takes significant time and effort to stay aware of economic and political developments. From an economic viewpoint, keeping social awareness has a significant opportunity cost, at least in terms of abandoned opportunities to do something else. Therefore, spending time and effort to stay aware, and voting in the elections accordingly, only makes sense if it eventually makes a difference. And if it will not make a difference, why should one bother to care to stay aware ?

Before proceeding further with the analysis of the situation, it is crucial to clarify what is meant by difference. If the individual has adequate social awareness and votes for a candidate who will best serve the interests of the individual, that is the right candidate for that individual and therefore -if elected- will create a positive value for the individual. But if the individual has inadequate social awareness and votes for a candidate who will serve others' interests at the expense of those of the individual, that is a wrong candidate for that individual and therefore -if elected- will create a negative value for the individual. In aggregate, as the society is made up of the individuals, if most of the society manage to vote for the right candidate for themselves, the outcome will be beneficial for the society and therefore will create a positive value for the society. However, if most of the society fails in their judgement and vote for a wrong candidate, the outcome will be harmful for the society and therefore will create a negative value for the society.

Needless to say, in practise, every positive result for the society does not necessarily mean a positive result for each and every individual, and vice versa. However, for the sake of this analysis on the significance of social awareness, assume that there are only two candidates, one right-candidate with the ability and goodwill to serve most of the society's interests in the best possible manner, and one wrong-candidate who is an extremist-populist willing to establish an autocracy-in-disguise and serve primarily the interests of himself and a group of Cheaters supporting him.

Coming back to the analysis of the appropriate decision for an individual on whether he should stay aware in spite of the high cost of staying aware or just not bother, the situation comes out to be a classical dilemma well known in game theory. Consider the table below, where the rows and columns show how the individual and the society may behave, and the values in the cells show the potential benefit (or, harm if the value is negative) they will face accordingly.

	SOCIETY CARES	SOCIETY DOES NOT CARE
INDIVIDUAL CARES	society : +10 individual : +10	society : -15 individual : - 20
INDIVIDUAL DOES NOT CARE	society : +10 individual : +15	society : -15 individual : -15

In the table, it is assumed that, the benefit of getting the right result at the election (i.e. the right political candidate winning the election) is assumed to be +15 for everybody (i.e. both the individual and the society), while getting the wrong result (i.e. the wrong candidate winning the election) costs -15. The cost of caring to stay aware (and thus voting for the right candidate) is -5 for everybody, while not caring incurs no cost.

In the case where both the individual and the society care, they both get a net benefit of +10 (benefit of +15 for the right result, minus cost of caring).

In the case where the individual does not care but the rest of the society cares, the individual gets the whole +15 benefit without incurring any cost, and the society still gets +10. This is the free-riding case for the individual, his most preferred option, as he does not bother to care at all but gets maximum benefit out of the election result, thanks to the caring of the society.

In the case where the individual cares but the rest of the society does not, the individual is harmed both by the wrong result (-15) and also incurs the cost of caring (-5), ending up at -20, and the society also gets -15 without incurring any cost of caring. This is the nightmare case for the individual, where he wasted time and effort, but still has to bear with the wrong result because the society did not bother to care.

Finally, in the case where neither the individual nor the society care, they both get -15, incurring no costs of caring.

To see how the individual will behave under the facts given in this table, consider his best options under each choice for the rest of the society. If the society cares, it is better for the individual not to care, as he will maximise his benefit to +15. If the society does not care, it is still better for the individual not to care, because this way he will at least minimise his harm to -15. Therefore, independent of how the rest of the society choses to behave, it seems best for the individual not to care to stay aware of the economic and political developments.

The implicit flawed assumption behind this logic is that the behaviour of the individual does not change the behaviour of the society. However, as every society is the collection of all of its individual members, when each individual runs this logic, nobody will care and the lose-lose case (where both the individual and the society lose -15) will come out, as the terrible but sustainable equilibrium.

In an intellectually-adult society, everybody knows that the society is the collection of its members, and thus only when each and every individual cares, the society will care by definition, and the win-win case (where both the individual and the society win +10) will result. This is the correct sustainable equilibrium that an intellectually-adult society has to reach and protect.

To reemphasize, *in an intellectually-adult society, each individual should be aware that the only way to reach the win-win case is to bother to care on a personal basis*, rather than trying to free ride on others. In other words, the society, being a collection of its members, can not behave any differently from its members by definition, and thus there is no free riding opportunity for the masses, apart from a few. And if very many members of the society try to fit into that free-riding few to maximise their own benefit, eventually most of the society will not care and all will end up at the lose-lose case.

SHOULD ONE VOTE IF ONE DOES NOT CARE TO STAY AWARE?

From a rational viewpoint, if an individual does not bother to care to stay aware or is not able to do so for whatever reason, it is best for the society if he does not bother to vote either. This way, at least he will not dilute the weight of the votes that are given by those who care to stay aware. *The worst behaviour is not-caring-but-voting*, simply because *when an individual does not care, he does not vote arbitrarily, but just becomes an easy prey for manipulation by the Cheaters*, and then by voting he serves the interests of the Cheaters against the interests of the society and thus against the interests of his own. If those who do not care are at least wise enough not to vote either, those who care to stay aware will have more weight in the election results and may save the society, including those who do not care. The danger here is that, if the individuals who lost their social awareness are not even aware that they have lost it, they will continue to vote – even if they understand and accept the logic above.

THE EMERGING DANGER

Assume that the individuals in the society know that they should keep their social awareness as high as possible and are prepared to incur the cost of doing it. The emerging danger here is that, the cost of staying aware is rising every passing day, and in spite of all their goodwill, many individuals may simply not be able to pay for that cost anymore.

During the recent decades, the cost of staying aware rose significantly for two separate but simultaneous reasons. First, the speed of rise in the complexity of the world around us reached unprecedented levels, due to factors like technological developments, globalisation, etc. - and that has increased the total amount of time and effort required to stay aware. Second, the opportunity cost of allocating even the same amount of time and effort as before has also risen, due to factors like the necessity of allocating more effort to surviving the day, or the distraction of attention to irrelevant issues including new ways of technological entertainment like social networks etc. These two reasons multiply out to result in an unbearable cost for many individuals.

If the society can not cure these troubles in time, it may lose social awareness not because it is not willing to keep it, but just because it will not be able to keep it anymore. This time, the terrible but sustainable equilibrium that emerges when nobody cares can be reached through the inability to care rather than the unwillingness to care. But the end result, namely the loss of welfare for the society, and eventually the destruction of the social order, will not change.

4.3 Manipulating The Political Opinion Of The Society

Who Wants To Manipulate Whom ?

When politics is considered, the primary suspects for the manipulation of the opinion of the society are assumed to be the politicians, as they are usually pre-sentenced to be guilty of trying to get themselves elected through misguiding the society by whatever means.

Even though the politicians are the primary suspects, they are neither the only nor the most important ones. *The real powerful and determined manipulator is the Cheating (Economic) Elite, who try to misguide the society to either support the policies that will serve the Cheaters' interests, or at least to elect the politicians whom the Cheating Elite can easily misguide (due to their lack of ability) or buyout (due to their lack of goodwill)* to serve their own interests at the expense of the society. Unfortunately, the Cheating Elite can inflict more harm on the society than the politicians, as the society is usually aware that it has to question the information flow from the politicians, while it is almost defenceless against all the misinformation originating from other sources supported by the Cheating Elite.

To see how and why manipulation works, it is necessary to keep in mind that the behaviour of intellectually-adults and the intellectually-children differ significantly in their decision making process on any economic or political issue.

Intellectually-adults, if they know a social issue, are also aware that they know, so they may take an active role in any relevant discussion to influence the others and when the time comes make their own decisions. If they don't know an issue, at least they are aware that they don't know, so they stay silent and try to learn about the issue by listening to reliable experts before they make their choice.

Intellectually-children don't know much about any social issue, and to make matters worse, they are not aware that they do not know. In some cases, they may naively believe that they know[7], but in most cases they are deliberately made to believe by the Cheaters that they know. In any case, they see no need to learn anything on the issue while they feel free to comment on and make a lot of noise, and finally act on their own judgement in making their final decision which naturally happens to benefit somebody else rather than themselves.

Within the intellectually-adults there are both the Fair Players and the Cheaters. The intellectually-children are actually the innocents, who are sometimes saved by the Fair Players but most of the times fall prey to Cheaters.

Consider an issue on which the society will collectively decide on. Assume that there are only two choices, such that, one maximises the society's interest, and the other benefits only a minority within the society, namely the Cheaters, but harms the society at large.

The Cheaters know that their target is the intellectually-children whom they need to manipulate to support the choice that benefits the Cheaters. They first try to silence the Fair Players, or when silencing is not possible, make so much noise that the voice of the Fair Players will not be heard much by the intellectually-children - who are not inclined to look for or listen to any complicated rational analysis anyway.

Next the Cheaters try to divert the attention of the intellectually-children on another misguiding issue that is only marginally relevant (if at all) to the real issue under consideration, but nicely packaged with it and presented as if there is a strong causation in between, such that if the intellectually-children base their choices on the misguiding issue, which happens to benefit the Cheaters, the main issue will also be solved. Meanwhile, although the Fair Players also have the freedom to communicate to the intellectually-children, their chances of success are relatively much smaller. This is simply because the Cheaters are usually bright enough to integrate a misguiding issue such that it is easy to understand and difficult to oppose (as it touches the feelings of the intellectually-children), and is mostly not totally wrong but just irrelevant. Selling such a simple but strong issue by easy-to-understand-and-easy-to-remember slogans is not difficult for the Cheaters, but explaining that something that is correct is actually irrelevant can not easily be done by such simple slogans and requires longer discussions. And intellectually-children do not like spending time on listening to competing ideas in length. The Cheaters, therefore, mostly beat the Fair Players and succeed in getting the support of the intellectually-children for the choice that benefits the Cheaters. Needless to say, the success of the Cheaters in manipulating the society's opinion will increase exponentially as the society's Social Intellect weakens.

Further Techniques Of Manipulation In Politics

RISING ASYMMETRY OF INFORMATION AND FALLING SOCIAL AWARENESS

Social awareness requires several conditions to be met simultaneously, namely, having access to complete and correct information on major social issues, social education and experience to analyse this information, and continuously allocating time and effort to gather and analyse such information. Unfortunately, on the one hand, the complexity of the world and the flow of information have risen exponentially, while on the other hand, the processing power of the human brain, the social education and experience, and the time and effort allocated to be socially aware have all stayed the same (or at best marginally improved) in almost all societies. These together have driven the asymmetry of information to sky high and the relative ability of most individuals in understanding the world to rock bottom, thus weakening their Social Intellect and eventually converting them to intellectually-children.

The Cheating Elite love to see that the society on average becomes and remains intellectually-childish and thus socially unaware, so that misguiding the society towards their own benefits will be much easier and can be done in a sustainable way. Therefore, the Cheating Elite happily support this natural problem of loss of relative intellect, at every possible stage.

The starting point for social awareness, namely social education, has been heavily guarded against widespread access, knowing well that any leak of information will be riskless for the Cheating Elite as long as the society remains intellectually incapable of processing that information. The establishment of a social education system for the society at large has not even been discussed as an issue of major importance in any media or any political arena, and there are no applications in practise apart from a few weak examples of limited civic education in a few societies.

In spite of this check point, the exponential rise in the flow of information has not escaped the attention of the Cheating Elite either. Another condition for social awareness, namely reaching correct and complete information, has also been crippled, not through classic means of censorship, but through flooding the environment with irrelevant or misguiding or simply junk information, among which it becomes very difficult to find out reliable vital information for developing social awareness.

Finally, to maximise the delight of the Cheaters, the third condition for social awareness, namely allocating time and effort to issues of major social importance, has became more difficult to abide by itself : as time and effort are limited resources for every individual, allocating them to social issues carries the opportunity cost of not allocating them elsewhere, and therefore, any rise in the opportunity cost of giving up on other issues will help to direct attention away from the social ones. As mentioned before, one such issue which is unavoidable for many individuals, is the necessity of allocating more time and effort to surviving the day as economic conditions worsen. Another issue that steals the time of most individuals, however, is not that difficult to avoid, but is still given priority above major social ones.

If there were a society which had solved its major economic and political issues completely and successfully, attained an optimal welfare level with high average incomes within acceptable inequality, and thus has ample free time for fun, then it makes perfect sense to for its members to engage their attention heavily in entertainment and sports activities, as both of these increase individuals' happiness tremendously. However, if a society still has many major economic and political issues to be solved, all with a potential to go worse if left untreated, then, first, spending too much time and material resources on entertainment and sports is a waste of society's limited potential, and second, sparing too much attention to them practically becomes a distraction of attention from the major issues that need to be solved. Thus, involvement in entertainment and sports, while a necessary activity for the happiness of the society for sure, and a very innocent one on the surface, becomes a source of harm to the long-term welfare of the society when exaggerated under inappropriate conditions. Although these distractors of attention may not be primarily promoted by the Cheaters, their excessive-consumption, especially by the intellectually-children, serve the Cheaters' purposes well.

PERCEPTION MANAGEMENT BY THE POLITICIANS

In principle, it is expected that politicians will focus on the social issues of critical importance for the society and reveal why they are different and superior to their rivals on those issues and thus how they will increase the welfare of the society if they get elected. However, in practise, politicians frequently borrow the basic principles of perception management from economics and apply them to politics in competing with their rivals. *They try to focus the society's attention to issues in which they believe they have an edge against their rivals or their rivals have relative weaknesses, even though those issues may not be the most critical ones for the welfare of the society under the prevailing conditions at that specific time. Similarly, they may try to shift focus away from issues of critical importance for the society, if they believe they have a weakness there or their rivals have some relative strength.* Again, as is the usual case in perception management, they present correct but incomplete or irrelevant and thus misguiding information. In that regard such behaviour is not illegal, or even only marginally unethical as long as no lies are involved, but definitely harmful for the society's welfare, as it shifts attention from the critical issues. Therefore, *it is in the best interest of the society to keep the focus on issues of real importance and resist to the diversion of discussion to irrelevant or less important issues*. But unfortunately, the weaker the society's Social Intellect gets, the more difficult will be to achieve this.

HIDING THE BEST OPTION

One common technique that the politicians of the older decades utilized frequently in societies with low Social Intellect, was *presenting only the options which either serve their own purposes or are totally unacceptable, thus leaving their desired option as the only practical choice.*

One well known way of doing this, practically used by the extremist politicians of the distant past, is hiding the balanced options as if they don't exist and presenting only the extremes, such that, on one extreme they stand themselves and the other extreme is even worse and thus totally unacceptable. The balanced option, which will dominate both extremes if presented, is carefully hidden and left out of discussion. For instance, in many cases in history, societies were presented the two extreme options for their economic system, the hard-core-socialism versus wild-capitalism, while the best option, a Free Market Economy with proper regulation and fair competition, was hidden with utmost care. Such approaches work well until the society becomes intellectual enough to realize that there is almost always a balanced option which dominates the extremes and demands to be presented that. It directly follows that once the society becomes intellectual enough, it starts to demand moderate policies promoted by mainstream politicians, rather than choosing among extremists or populists. However, that still may not be enough.

Even when the society is aware that the solution is at some shade of grey between the white and the black, there are still many shades of grey between the two, and the optimal solution is only at one of them.

For instance, every society, in their social system, needs to balance the personal interests of the individuals versus the interests of the society on the one hand, and the short-term interests of both versus the long-term interests of both, on the other. It is amazing to see how spectacularly societies failed to balance them most of the times, even in the most recent decades.

From the perspective of perception management, the critical issue here is whether the society is presented the optimal shade of grey at all, or was just made to choose between say a darker shade of grey versus the extremes. Once again, this happens when the beneficiary of the dark grey option tries to guide the society towards its own preference, by hiding the light grey option, where the optimal solution lies. And again, as the society increases its Social Intellect further, it realizes that there are more than one shades of grey and demands to be presented all.

And it should now be clear what happens if the Social Intellect of the society starts to weaken again, as has been happening in the recent decades. The options at the extremes, mostly presented by the populists, will once again start to emerge as possible remedies to society's troubles, while the moderate paths will fall out of attention.

The rest of this story, which will not be a pleasant one, will continue at Section 4.6. Before that, however, some issues regarding the agency problems in politics have to be examined to complete the picture.

4.4   Voters' Inability To Evaluate Politicians And Policies

The Voter As The Principal

In a democracy, the principal (society) - agent (politician) relation is at the heart of the political system.

As explained in Section 3.3, in a system based on an agency relationship, the success of the system not only depends on the ability and goodwill of the agent (politician), but also on the average intellectual level of the principal (society), simply because the principal's proper evaluation of the performance of the agent is a necessity for the flawless functioning of the system. The principal, based on its evaluation of the agent on his past performance, will determine whether to keep or replace the agent in the future. And even if the past performance of the current agent is satisfactory, based on his evaluation of all available candidates, the principal may decide that the potential performance of another agent will be better in the future and a change will be beneficial. Reading backwards, if the principal fails to make a proper evaluation, even if the past performance of the current agent is inadequate, and even if the potential performance of another agent will be better in the future, the principal may still fail to make a change and will have to bear the negative consequences of his wrong choice. Therefore, *unless the principal is intellectual enough to choose the right agent, having qualified agents in the political arena is of no use*.

In a democracy, therefore, the main critical assumption is that the principal has the ability to choose the right agent. And the fuse in the system is that, in case the principal fails to make a right choice occasionally, he can change the agent in the next round of elections. However, what is the use of having the chance to change the agent in the next round, if the principal continues to elect one wrong agent after another? The fuse in the system works to protect the principal against mis-choices that are supposed to happen rarely. It simply can not protect the principal from his permanent deficiency of Social Intellect.

Some classic cases of failure of the principal in making choices in a democracy that are common in intellectually-childish societies are worth a closer look.

Voters Making Decisions Looking Backward

In an intellectually-childish society, voters do not elect the next agents (politicians for the Execution and the Legislation) based on forward looking evaluations of all candidates, but rather to reward or punish the existing one, looking backwards. If they are happy with their existing agents and their current policies, they vote for their continuation even if there may now be better candidates with superior policies. And if they are not happy, they make a change even if the other available candidates lack the potential to be better or are actually worse. Thus, the voters, as the principal, vote based on their happiness in the past for which the existing agent is held responsible, rather than their potential happiness in the future which may or may not be improved by another candidate. And this is one front where democracy fails in an intellectually-childish society, as a rational voter is supposed to elect the candidate who has the best potential to serve the society in the future, independent of the past performance of the existing agent.

VOTERS' FAILURE IN EVALUATING PAST PERFORMANCE

As if looking backward rather than forward is not enough as a major mistake, to maximise their misery, the voters in an intellectually-childish society usually fail to properly evaluate the past performance of the existing politicians.

Absolute Performance versus Relative Performance

In light of the concepts and the jargon introduced in Section 3.3, the eventual outcome (called the *absolute performance*) of a political policy pursued by a politician is a combined result of two sub-components: One is the inherent value of the applied policy (whether it is the correct policy or not) which is under the control of the politician, and the other is the external conditions under which the policy is executed which are totally beyond the control of the politician. Therefore, for the proper assessment of the inherent value of the applied policy, the eventual outcome has to be evaluated relative to the external conditions prevailing at that period. For that reason, the inherent value of the policy may also be called the *relative performance* of the policy.

These external conditions can be global, like the global growth rate, global changes in pricing of capital and availability of financing, changes in prices of commodities, etc., or local, like the changes in natural growth rate of the society depending on changes in the working age population, effects of the education system set decades ago by other politicians, the existence or non-existence of infrastructure investments made in the distant past by other politicians, the existence or non-existence of institutions that were established or neglected in the past, etc. The common attribute of these external conditions is that they are not under the control of the current politician and can not be altered in the short run, or at all.

The voter, as the principal, should keep in mind the effects of the external conditions while evaluating the politician, as his agent. However, taking external conditions into consideration is easier said than done. The complication arises from the fact that these external conditions should be evaluated in two dimensions, namely their *stability* and their *neutrality*.

In principle, in setting his policies the politician has to take into consideration the existing and expected external conditions, so that the best outcome for the society can be achieved. In practise, this may only be possible if the external conditions are stable or rationally forecastable. However, sometimes comes a major change that could not have been foreseen, which dominates the eventual outcome. In such cases there is nothing that any politician could have done. An intellectually-adult society should understand that a change in the eventual outcome due to such an unforecastable major change in the external conditions is neither a failure nor a success of the politician.

Even when the external conditions are somewhat stable or rationally forecastable, they may or may not be neutral. The external conditions are sometimes neutral, such that their effect on the eventual outcome is minimal, and therefore the inherent value of the applied policy will be the prime determinant of the eventual outcome. In other words, the absolute performance of the politician will be a reflection of his relative performance. However, at other times there can be pretty strong headwinds or tailwinds, such that they dominate the eventual outcome independent of the policies applied by the politician. At times of strong headwinds, namely negative external conditions, the eventual outcome will be negative even if the applied policies are correct. Similarly, at times of strong tailwinds, namely positive external conditions, the eventual outcome will be positive even if the applied policies are wrong. Needless to say, correct policies applied at times of positive external conditions will create stellar performances and make the politicians heroes, while wrong policies applied at times of negative external conditions will have terrible consequences or may even create system failures.

Only the Past Relative Performance is an Indicator for the Future

As the external conditions are beyond the control of the politicians, the voters have to evaluate how good the politicians performed in relative terms, namely whether they have applied the correct policies, rather than focusing on the eventual outcome. The necessity of this approach is based on the fact that, as the *past relative performance* of the politician was under his control, it *is a very strong indicator of his future relative performance*, namely his expected success in case he is elected again. However, his past absolute performance (namely the eventual outcome in the past), partially or sometimes heavily depend on the external conditions beyond the control of the politician, and therefore is not an indicator of his future absolute performance in any way. Awareness of this crucial difference is the key for the success of the principal in making proper evaluations and decisions.

Evaluations by Intellectually-Adult versus Intellectually-Childish Societies

In intellectually-childish societies, voters consider the absolute change in their welfare in the past, without any reference to how it could have changed without the interference of the existing politicians, for the better or for the worse, and assume that this is a predictor of the absolute change in their welfare to be expected in the future. Thus, if the eventual outcome was positive, even if the applied policies were wrong, the politician will probably be offered a chance to run the system again. Similarly, if eventual outcome was negative, even if the applied policies were correct, the politician will probably not be offered another chance to run the system.

In intellectually-adult societies, voters consider the relative performance of the policies applied by the politician in reference to the external conditions, thus the politician will be evaluated independent of the eventual outcome. If he applied correct policies in the past, even if the eventual outcome was negative, he will be offered a chance to run the system again. Similarly, if he applied wrong policies in the past, even if the eventual outcome was positive, he will not be offered another chance to run the system.

A Simple Illustration

To illustrate the dynamics of eventual outcomes as a combined result of the external conditions and the applied policies, and the corresponding voter evaluations and decisions in different societies, consider the cases shown in the table below. For ease of analysis, numeric values are given to the effects of both the external conditions and the inherent value of policies applied by the politicians. Naturally, correct policies have a positive value added for the society, and the wrong policies have a negative value added. Similarly, changes in external conditions that are beneficial to the society (tailwinds) have positive values, and harmful ones (headwinds) have negative values.

For simplicity, assume that there are two contradictory policies applied by respective politicians, one with positive and the other with negative value added for the society, under any external condition. The society may alter between these two politicians and their policies depending on its decision criteria. The eventual outcome, naturally, is the sum of the effect of the external condition and the effect of the applied policy.

In cases where the effects of external conditions are weaker than those of the applied policy, like in the relatively closed and simple economies of the past (before the global economic integration and the technical developments of the last few decades), the eventual outcomes are dominated by the value of the applied policies, and thus, the absolute and the relative performances give equivalent results in terms of being successful or not.

In the table below, which examines all possible cases under this assumption, the effects of external conditions are shown by +/-5 (beneficial ones positive), and effect of applied policies are shown by +/- 15 (correct policies positive).

Effect of External Conditions	Effect of Inherent Value of Policy (Relative Performance)	Eventual Outcome (Absolute Performance)	Evaluation of Intellectually Adult Society	Evaluation of Intellectually Childish Society
+5	+15	+20	Positive	Positive
+5	-15	-10	Negative	Negative
-5	+15	+10	Positive	Positive
-5	-15	-20	Negative	Negative

Although the evaluation criteria of the intellectually-childish society, namely absolute performance, and that of the intellectually-adult society, namely relative performance, are different, under the assumption of the effects of applied policy dominating the effects of external conditions, the results of evaluations of both societies come out to be the same. In both societies, the policy with positive value added is kept once found and thus the politician is re-elected, and the policy with negative value added is changed and thus the politician is replaced with another candidate in the next elections. Thus, in both societies the system works in the way it should. Therefore, as it mostly happened in the past, when the effects of external conditions are weaker than those of the applied policies, democracy had a chance to give the right result even if the society was intellectually-childish and had the wrong evaluation approach based on absolute performance.

The story, however, has been changing in the recent decades. As technological advancements continue and global social and/or economic integration proceeds, the effects of any major development in any society spills over to all other societies, much more than they have ever done in the past. This practically means that external conditions start to become dominant on the eventual outcomes for each and every society.

This change makes the evaluation of the value of applied policies, and thus the relative performance of the politicians, much more important, as wrong evaluations will now have very negative consequences for a society.

The table below examines all the possible cases under dominant external conditions, where the effects of external conditions are now shown by +/- 25 (beneficial ones positive), and effect of applied policies are still +/-15 (correct policies positive).

	Effect of External Conditions	Effect of Inherent Value of Policy (Relative Performance)	Eventual Outcome (Absolute Performance)	Evaluation of Intellectually Adult Society	Evaluation of Intellectually Childish Society
A	+25	+15	+40	Positive	Positive
B	+25	-15	+10	Negative	Positive
C	-25	+15	-10	Positive	Negative
D	-25	-15	-40	Negative	Negative

The intellectually-adult society evaluates the politician on the inherent value of his policy, therefore, on his relative success with respect to external conditions, and not on the absolute outcome. Thus, the society re-elects the politician on Cases A and C, and replaces him on Cases B and D. Notice that at Case C, the eventual outcome is negative, but as the inherent value of the applied policy is positive, the society re-elects the politician in spite of the eventual outcome, considering that relative to what could have been done, the policy still added value. Also notice that at Case B, the eventual outcome is positive, but as the inherent value of the applied policy is negative, the society replaces the politician in spite of the eventual outcome, considering that relative to what could have been done, the policy caused a significant loss of value.

The intellectually-childish society, however, evaluates the politician, and thus his policy, based on the absolute outcome. Thus, it re-elects the politician on Cases A and B, and replaces him on Cases C and D. Notice that at Cases B and C, it reacts in just the opposite ways of an intellectual-adult society.

The Long-Term Implications on Growth and Stability

Although both societies behave the same at Cases A and D, the differences on Cases B and C lead to very different futures for each society in the long-term.

Consider the intellectually-adult society. After experiencing a Case C type of period, during which external conditions are very negative but correct policies are applied by the politician to minimize the inescapable damage, the society will re-elect the existing politician. As a result, when external conditions get better, say in the following period, combined with the correct policies, they face very positive outcomes and make up for their loss, so they experience Case A. For illustrative purposes, assume that external conditions stay volatile, and reach positive and negative extremes at equal frequencies. Then, the intellectually-adult society will face another negative external conditions period next, namely C, but stick to the correct policies again. And still sticking to the correct policies, they will next face Case A again, and so on. Therefore, the intellectually-adult society will toggle between Cases A and C, but avoid Cases B and D. Thus, their long-term average absolute performance will be the average of the outcomes of these two cases, namely in a four year period [-10 +40 -10 +40] / 4 = +15. Notice that, in spite of the dominance of the external conditions at all times, the intellectually-adult society's long-term average performance will be equal to the value added by the applied correct policies, namely the relative performance of the politician, as effects of positive and negative external conditions will cancel out each other in the long-term.

Consider the intellectually-childish society now. After experiencing a Case C period, during which external conditions are very negative but correct policies are applied by the politician to minimize the inescapable damage, the society will still replace the existing policies with the opposite policies, which are wrong by definition of the illustration. As a result, next they will face Case B, where positive external conditions will be wasted by the wrong policies. However, as the eventual outcome is positive in Case B, they will re-elect the existing politician with the wrong policies, to face Case D next, where the wrong policies coupled with negative external conditions will result in a very negative eventual outcome. So, this time they will replace the politician, and next enjoy Case A, where the correct policies meet positive external conditions, to give a very positive eventual outcome. So they continue to re-elect the existing politician, and next face Case C again. This restarts the chain reaction again and continue in the same order: B, D, A, C... Therefore, the long-term average absolute performance will be the average of the outcomes of these four cases, namely [-10 +10 -40 +40] / 4 = 0. Notice that, due to the misguiding effect of the dominance of external conditions on the eventual outcomes on which the intellectually-childish society bases its decisions at all times, the society frequently makes wrong evaluations. Thus, the long-term performance of the society comes out to be zero, which actually is still equal to the aggregate value added by the applied correct and wrong policies - namely the positive and negative relative performances of the politicians eventually cancelling out each other, while the effects of positive and negative external conditions also cancel out each other in the long-term.

A vital observation is that, the intellectually-childish society gets the right evaluations for the wrong reasons in two out of the four cases above, namely at Cases A and D. Thus, from their viewpoint, their system seems to perform well sometimes, and just randomly fail at some other times.

But in fact, as illustrated and explained above, there is nothing random in this mis-performance, and as long as they remain intellectually-childish their long-term performance will never be good.

This simple illustration shows that *the intellectually-adult society, which evaluates the past performances thinking in relative terms, namely considering what has actually been achieved under the applied policy versus what could have been achieved (with another policy) under the prevailing external conditions, and thus makes the correct evaluations, develops in a sustainable fashion.* On the contrary, the intellectually-childish society, which evaluates the past performances by only considering the eventual outcomes, namely the absolute performances, just experiences many short-term fluctuations, without any long-term development.

And a further observation is vital regarding the worst case scenarios. Notice that the intellectually-childish society will sooner or later face Case D where the absolute performance will be catastrophic (-40), and may even cause a total system breakdown, ruining the welfare of the society. The intellectually-adult society, however, at worst faces Case C (-10) under negative outside conditions, which is much easier to handle while keeping the system up and running.

To clarify again, the key to these differences is that, the relative performance of the politician in the past is a valid indicator of his potential relative performance in the future, as policy setting is under his control. And a bright politician stays to be bright. And thus comes a sustainable long-term development in the intellectually-adult societies who base their decisions on relative performances. However, the absolute performance of the politician in the past, mostly dominated by the external conditions, is not a valid indicator of his potential absolute performance in the future, as external conditions are not under his control. Thus comes just randomness and no sustainable long-term development in the intellectually-childish societies who base their decisions on absolute performances. Therefore, *politicians* should not be evaluated on the basis of the eventual outcomes, but *should only be evaluated on the basis of what is under their control, namely the inherent value of their policies. A fact easily forgotten if and when the society starts to lose its Social Intellect.*

A Closer Look At The Recent Decades

To recapitulate, the discussion above reveals two causation relations. On the one hand, in the simple world of the distant past where the effect of the external conditions was marginal relative to the effect of the applied policies, democracy worked well even for the intellectually-childish societies. However, under the rising complexity of the recent decades, the effect of the external conditions may sometimes dominate the effect of the applied policies, and then democracy starts to fail the in intellectually-childish societies.

On the other hand, as the complexity of the world rises, as it has been happening in the recent decades, societies' Social Intellect starts to weaken, and unless proper precautions are taken in time, every society will eventually convert to an intellectually-childish one.

Taken together, *the rise in the complexity of the world necessitates a high Social Intellect for democracies to function properly, but simultaneously weakens the Social Intellect of all societies.* Therefore, the rise in the complexity of the world in the recent decades is enough to create a breakdown in both economic and political systems unless major precautions are taken to rise back the Social Intellect of the societies.

Voters Making Decisions Looking Forward

An intellectually-adult voter is supposed to elect the candidate who has the best potential to serve the society in the future, independent of what has happened in the past with others. Although intellectually-adult societies are still missing in practise, some societies do look forward from time to time, either because they eventually come to realize that there is a need for a significant change in the classic policies, or simply because some politicians closely paired with certain policies choose to retire by their own decision (or just because they happen to be mortal). In both cases, there is a need for fresh politicians and fresh policies, without any track records, making it necessary to look forward.

An intellectually-adult society will base its forward-looking choice on the merit and goodwill of the candidates, and on the rationality of their promises and policies. Once the society makes a right choice, it finds itself in Cases A or C of the illustration above, and starts its regular toggling. It is possible that the society may sometimes make a mistake in its choice and find itself at Cases B or D, however, as they can evaluate a politician correctly once he is given the job, in the next round the society will change their choice and convert to Cases A or C again, without a major long-term trouble.

The intellectually-childish society, however, will probably face trouble in making the right choice. On the one hand, there will be dream-sellers, including all sorts of populists, whose main strategy is to promise to immediately deliver the impossible to satisfy the colourful dreams of the society. Such promises are mostly self-contradictory, like paying low taxes but getting infinite social security and perfect social infrastructure, etc. But for the intellectually-childish voter, such fast and easy solutions are difficult to resist to believe in. And in cases where even the intellectually-childish voter can not be made to believe in the existence of any easy solution, extremists will emerge in different shapes. They may turn out to be revenge-sellers, promoting the idea that if the losers of the current system can not be made to win, then at least the winners of the current system should be made to lose with them. Or they may turn out to be fear-traders, arguing that the very existence of the individual and the society is in danger due to a heavily exaggerated and mispresented risk, and the only path to survival passes through electing the extremist politician himself.

On the other hand, there may still be candidates with the ability and goodwill required for serving the best interest of the society, however, without fast and easy solutions. They stick to rationality and to the bare realities that are not so nice to hear, and can only offer real solutions that are difficult to implement and thus give fruit only in the long-term, requiring various sorts of sacrifices from the society in the short-term.

Naturally, intellectually-childish societies will usually prefer to believe in the dream-sellers and their beautiful promises that caress their irrationally high expectations, and thus will next find themselves in Cases B or D of the illustration above. And as long as they remain intellectually-childish and keep up believing in forward looking empty promises, they will toggle between the Cases B and D, inevitably ruining their future.

Notice that this is even worse than the situation assumed in the toggling-between-opposite-policies scenario in the illustration above regarding looking backwards, as in that case even the intellectually-childish society will experience Cases A and C once in a while. Similarly, making choices on a random basis would have been better, as the society might once in a while elect some rational politician by mere luck. Thus, *the worst possible case is when an intellectually-childish society tries to make forward looking choices, but buys the irrational policies of the dream-sellers over and over again*.

Therefore, although making choices looking forward is the best approach in principle, it also requires an intellectually advanced society, and preferably an intellectually-adult one, to succeed in practise. Otherwise, it may end up to be the worst approach for the society.

In short, whether the society is looking backward or forward in making political choices, better long-term outcomes are obtained as the intellectual level of the society rises. And unfortunately the opposite is also valid: *the right to decide one's own future in a democracy is a great feeling, however, if done without having the necessary intellectual background, it ends up in selecting the wrong future*.

The Need For An Honest Diagnosis

Individuals like to look for a guilty figure apart from themselves whenever they face trouble. Following that fashion, in the years following the economic troubles faced during 2008 and on, many societies felt betrayed by their existing economic and political systems, namely Free Market Economy and Democracy, believing that a totally different but much better social order, preferably one from outer space, can be established to cure all the troubles, without any need for the individuals to bother to improve their own selves, namely their intellectual level.

It will help any society to keep in mind that, *within the prevailing western social order, when something starts to go wrong in the economy, something must have been going wrong in the political system way before that.* This in turn means that something must be going wrong in the principal-agent relationship within the democratic system, and, as is the usual case in agency relations, it follows that *the primary trouble lies with the principal in the relation, namely the individuals making up the society.*

As the primary trouble lies with the society, the solution has to initiate there too, starting with preventing the weakening of the Social intellect of the society, and if possible, increasing the intellectual level of the society in time. That, unfortunately, is neither an easy nor a quick solution. But it is the only solution.

4.5   The Political Agents

High Expectations From Political Agents

In the agency relation in politics, the politician is the agent of the society who is expected to make decisions on behalf of the society but in a much better and advanced way than the society itself can make, to protect and promote the interests of the society and to maximise its long-term welfare. And such high expectations are not limited to the top Legislative and Executive functions, but also cover the rest of the state bureaucracy who may be considered as indirect agents of the society.

INABILITY, INEFFICIENCY AND THE STATE

During the latest decades, fuelled by the domination of economic thinking by neo-liberalistic principles, the state started to be considered as a burden on the society, based on two arguments. First, the performance of the state in fulfilling its basic duties regarding the economy, including the regulation of the markets, is so unsuccessful that many times it introduces more harm than good to the economy, and thus it may be better if the state does not regulate much at all. Second, the state works so inefficiently that it consumes too many resources with respect to the value it produces for the society. It naturally follows that, the size of the state has to be minimized as much as possible.

Such scaling down, coupled with the minimization of the regulatory power of the state, however, happens to enable widespread cheating and cause a significant decrease in competition in many major markets, which in turn decreases the welfare of the society. This makes the scaling down of the state a very convenient development for the Cheaters and naturally gets their full support. However, an intellectually-adult society should be able to find better solutions.

The primary concern regarding the state should not be the size of the state within an economy, but its efficiency and its ability to produce economic and social value for the society. If the state were as efficient and as capable as the private sector, the society would not have needed to worry about its size, and the state could have been allowed to grow as much as necessary -no less and no more- to play its vital roles, including that of the regulator of the markets. To reemphasize, this does not mean that an efficient state should get as large as possible, but just on the contrary, *the state should still not go beyond the bare necessities required to properly fulfil its main functions. However, the coverage of bare necessities is not as narrow as advertised in many societies during the latest decades*, as the many resulting troubles have revealed.

Therefore, the critical question is why the state happens to be less capable and less efficient than the private sector.

POLITICAL AGENTS' FAILURE TO MEET HIGH EXPECTATIONS

A natural reason for the perceived failure of the state is the failure of the political agents to live up to the high expectations of the society. The agents usually lack either the ability or the goodwill, or both, and thus naturally fail to run the system and the state in the best possible way, even if they were left to their own.

And in practise, they are rarely left to their own. They are almost always exposed to the efforts of the Cheaters to persuade them either to mis-regulate the markets to the benefit of the Cheaters, or to mis-allocate the resources of the state (and thus the society) directly to the Cheaters. Therefore, the Cheaters also care about the ability and the goodwill of the politicians and the state bureaucrats, except that they want just the opposite of what the society needs. The Cheaters want the politicians and the state bureaucrats to be easy preys, such that the politicians and bureaucrats should either lack the necessary ability not to be fooled by the misguidance of the Cheaters, or should lack the necessary goodwill to stand against the benefits offered to them by the Cheaters.

It is therefore critical to correctly diagnose the root cause of the trouble here. First, the frequent failure of the state is because of the lack of the ability or the goodwill of the politicians and the bureaucrats who run the state. Second, as a side effect that makes matters even worse, this lack of high-quality human resources in politics and bureaucracy makes the political system and the state vulnerable to Cheaters. Third, and the most important of all, *it is primarily the fault of the society (as the principal) to fail to attract and elect the human resources that can fulfil their high expectations as their political agents.*

Therefore, as the society advances intellectually, in addition to improving its capability of evaluating its political agents, it should focus on *maximising the quality of human resources attracted to politics and bureaucracy*, so that the performance of the state will rise, and thus the state can be let to grow as much as needed to maximise the welfare of the society.

Patriotism, Rationality And The Cheaters

Every society needs politicians and bureaucrats with both ability and goodwill. And the case for ability is clear: as the complexity of the world rises, it gets ever harder to have adequate ability to deal with the political issues. Thus, a politician has to be exceptionally wise and rational, and has to have advanced Social Education and years of accumulated experience.

The case for goodwill, however, is more complicated.

IRRATIONAL PATRIOTISM VERSUS RATIONAL GOODWILL

Throughout history, and even currently, in almost all societies, patriotism and goodwill are believed to be closely associated with each other, such that, patriotism is considered to be a solution for the required goodwill component of the agency relation inherent in democracies. Unfortunately, at least in practise, it is not.

To diagnose the trouble with this misunderstanding, it is necessary to clarify both concepts and then distinguish between the real requirement for a politician, namely *rational goodwill*, versus the wrong expectation of the society, namely *irrational patriotism*.

In *irrational patriotism*, the politician is expected to sacrifice his own being, including his own interests and potential welfare, for the good of the society under all conditions and at all times. Such an unconditional and inescapable sacrifice, unfortunately, does not sound rational to any wise individual in today's societies. It thus follows that, even if there are such patriots, as they most probably fail to satisfy the rationality component, they will lack the necessary ability to succeed in their mission. Therefore, the society in practise has one in a million chance to find a hero with both the desire to unconditionally sacrifice himself (for some personal reason beyond rationality) and the wisdom to succeed in serving the best interest of the society. And if there is separation of powers in the political system, as is the case in most democracies up to a certain extent, a single hero can not accomplish much by himself unless he is accompanied by many other heroes, making the situation a practical impossibility.

In rational goodwill, the politician is expected to serve the society with ability and goodwill, and to sacrifice his own interests if, but only if, necessary, and in return for his qualified service for the best interest of the society and the risk of potential sacrifice he is taking, he has to be both materially compensated and morally honoured. Becoming a politician under this scheme will be a rational choice for those who both desire it and are capable of it.

CHEATERS' PREFERENCE

The inclusion of politicians with both ability and goodwill to the political arena, through the scenario where they are compensated fairly for their service in both material and moral terms, will definitely promote the best interests of the society, including its protection against Cheaters.

As a natural consequence, the Cheating Elite are always keen to keep such people away from the political arena by keeping politics to be an unsuitable career for those with superior abilities. And this is most effectively done by promoting irrational patriotism as the foremost attribute of a politician, and intentionally mis-defining patriotism as sacrificing one's own interests and potential welfare even when there is no need to do so. And if the Cheaters succeed, as they mostly do in intellectually-childish societies, the society will fail to adequately compensate its politicians materially and morally, and thus driving away all the potential candidates with superior abilities, and leaving the political arena only to those who are lacking either the rationality and the ability to serve the society well, or the goodwill to do so, if not both.

To clarify, even if the politicians are all irrational patriots with the best of intensions for their society, their lack of rationality, and thus their lack of superior ability required today, will still make them incapable of protecting and promoting the interests of the society against those of the Cheaters. The other option, happily made available to the society by the Cheaters, is to elect politicians with superior ability, but without a sincere goodwill, so that even though they know that the society will not compensate them properly and fairly, they will create other ways to compensate themselves, most probably coupled with serving the interests of the Cheating Elite who supported them, at the expense of the society. And unfortunately, *intellectually-childish societies always fall into this trap, by accepting and demanding irrational patriotism as an undisputable precondition for being a politician, and thus condemning themselves to perpetually lose against the Cheating Elite, either by electing the incapables or the ill-willed as their political agents.*

THE NEED TO REDEFINE PATRIOTISM IN A RATIONAL FORM

An intellectually-adult society will redefine patriotism such that it embraces rationality and thus does not contradict with rational goodwill.

By natural definition, patriotism necessitates keeping the interests of the society above the interests of the politician at all times. However, this does not mean that patriotism is only keeping the interests of the society in mind, and sacrificing the politician's own interest unnecessarily, that is to say, even when they are not contradicting with those of the society. In other words, *rational patriotism permits to keep in mind both the interests of the society and the interests of the politician simultaneously, while placing the interests of the society above that of the politician only when they come into conflict.* To illustrate, this is similar to saying that, by the principle of rational patriotism, all military personnel should be willing to sacrifice their lives for the society in case a war breaks up - however, this does not mean that the military personnel should accept to be shot down to death after a few years in their career even if there is no reason to require that. Thus, *patriotism in a rational sense, is sacrificing oneself for the society if and only if it becomes necessary,* but not committing definite suicide of any sort without reason.

What all this means is that, any politician who would like to pass the patriotism test should not be required to sacrifice for sure his own material and moral interests, as sacrificing oneself for no reason is not an attractive option for any rational individual. Just on the contrary, the politician should know that the society will fairly appreciate and materially and morally compensate his service, so that he can stick to goodwill and serve the society well. Otherwise, as the Cheaters would like to see, only those with limited ability, meaning no potential to succeed in any other path, or worse, with the intention to cheat to gain riches, will choose to become politicians, and that scenario will not end well for the society.

Therefore, *if the society wants people with wisdom, superior ability and goodwill, including rational patriotism, to join the political arena, it should first make sure that politics will be a reliable and rational career for such people, including satisfying their moral and material needs as good as their other potential options outside politics or the state.*

A CLOSER LOOK AT LACK OF MATERIAL COMPENSATION

There is a famous saying in the corporate world: if you pay peanuts, you work with monkeys. Needless to say, the shareholders in the private sector, as the principals, are paying huge sums to their directors and managers, as their agents, not because they are too dumb to be able to cut costs, but rather because they are aware that what they pay is worth with respect to what they get. Fairly compensating the agent in return for his services for the principal is a bright idea.

Similarly, as politicians are the agents of the society in politics, compensating politicians materially will not be a waste of public resources. Just on the contrary, it will be a great use of public resources, as more capable and good-willed politicians will generate tremendous value for the society in two ways. First by promoting the interests of the society in the best possible ways and thus maximising the value created for the society through good political management. And second, by minimizing cheating against the society and thus minimising the harm inflicted on the society by the Cheaters. And the combination of these two will maximise the welfare of the society in the long run.

Unfortunately, partially due to their lack of Social Intellect and partially due to being misguided by the Cheaters, societies still insist on paying peanuts to their political agents (politicians and bureaucrats), naively believing that the agents are already heavily rewarded with the honour of sacrificing themselves for the society. And this understanding not only limits the value created by the political agents for the society, but also enables the Cheaters to easily misguide or buy out politicians and bureaucrats to act against the best interests of the society. The cumulative loss the society faces this way is multiples of scales higher than the savings it makes through limiting the material compensation of its political agents. And as the complexity of the world increases more and more, as is happening in the latest decades, the cumulative size of the loss of the society skyrockets. Unfortunately, while the compensation of the political agents is mostly transparent, it is impossible to observe the loss of the society explicitly, and thus a direct comparison can not be made easily. However, an intellectually-adult society can still figure out the scales of its loss versus its savings, through rational consideration. And for the intellectually-childish society, a simple analogy may help to illustrate the case: if an individual needs to go to a doctor and has to trust his life to the doctor's decisions, will he primarily search for the cheapest doctor? Or the most capable one? And how frequently do they happen to coincide?

PREFERENCES ON WHERE TO SAVE AND WHERE TO SPEND

As a matter of comedy, societies which still consider irrational patriotism as a precondition for entering politics and thus are very much against compensating their politicians materially and morally in an explicit manner, have absolutely no problem with tremendously over-paying and over-honouring celebrities in entertainment and sports. And as a matter of tragedy, while such celebrities may   at best have some limited contribution to the economic development of the society, they are in fact distracting the attention of the society away from significant issues in economics and politics, and thus unintentionally cause a decrease in the Social Intellect of the society, as discussed in Sections 4.2 and 4.3. It may be a good idea for the society to consider changing its preferences.

SOCIETY'S ABILITY TO ELECT THE RIGHT POLITICAL AGENTS

In principle, democracy is supposed to be choosing the best political agents among the good. But in practice, it became choosing the least bad among the bad. Quality of human resources in politics is therefore a major problem. As discussed above, the lack of fair material and moral compensation is one of the reasons, but it is not the only reason.

As discussed in Section 3.2, the so-called Lemons Theory introduced by George Akerlof states that, in economics bad assets drive good assets out of the market when the consumer is unable to differentiate between them, and thus comes a market failure. Similarly, politics is a lemons market where low-quality distracts high-quality. The inability of the voter to differentiate between the right and the wrong political agents, drives out the right ones, and paves the way for a political system failure.

As discussed in Section 4.4, when the voters are incapable of evaluating their political agents, they can neither reward nor punish them properly. And then, to the pleasure of the Cheaters, the carrots remain too little to motivate any individuals with superior potential and high moral values to consider a career in politics or bureaucracy, and the sticks remain too weak to demotivate those with limited ability or goodwill to stay away from politics or bureaucracy.

In today's complicated environment, even if a politician is highly capable and experienced, he still will not be able to make perfect decisions in all cases. In practice, even the best of talent and expertise can only reveal a statistical success, where the right decisions overweight the wrong decisions, making the overall picture a net success in the longer run. However, especially in the intellectually-childish societies, the media, both classic and social, happily misguided by the Cheating Elite, is ready to amplify any politician's statistically unavoidable mistakes, while neglecting or downgrading almost all his successes, without any urge to calculate the net balance for a fair evaluation. Thus, even those individuals with superior capabilities will not choose to join the political competition as they will fear that they will not be fairly evaluated and just get wasted in the lemons market of politics. Therefore, the intellectual level of the society plays a significant role in attracting or distracting superior talent to politics. And the more the society loses Social Intellect the more the talented agents will stay away from (or leave) politics.

It is therefore necessary to clarify that paying more to politicians will bring no benefit unless the society is intellectual enough to elect the agents with both ability and goodwill to political posts. *Only after the society develops its ability to make the right choice, better compensation of politicians in material and moral terms will attract individuals with superior ability and goodwill to politics*, and offer better options of choice to the society.

THE INTRA-SOCIETY BRAIN DRAIN

Any rational and bright individual who has spent many years of his lifetime educating himself and thus paved his way for a successful career, will naturally aim to create value for the society and get compensated fairly in return, both materially and morally, in a sustainable fashion. And such a career expectation, unfortunately, does not cover politics as an alternative, especially in intellectually-childish societies, for the reasons explained above.

In economics, a major trouble that developing societies face is the inter-society brain drain, where the well educated bright minds of the developing societies are attracted by the economically advanced societies, making life even harder for the developing ones. Similarly, in politics, *societies are experiencing an intra-society brain drain where their best educated and brightest minds are attracted by their private sector*, rather than by their public sector, thus preventing the formation of a better Legislation, Execution and bureaucracy that will serve the best interests of these societies.

And the cure for that trouble is clear. First, the societies will improve their ability to properly evaluate their political agents, which in turn will enable them to elect the right political agents. And next, they will better compensate their political agents materially and morally, and thus attract some of their best and brightest minds to politics. And then, democracy will at least overcome one major obstacle on its way to success.

Politicians And Excessive Risk Taking

Sometimes the abilities of the politicians currently on duty are simply not adequate for success. In the jargon of the previous section's analysis, their policies come out to be so wrong and thus their relative performance is so negative that the eventual outcome (their absolute performance) definitely comes out to be negative.

And sometimes, although the politicians currently on duty apply the right policies (i.e. their relative performance is positive) the prevailing or unexpectedly changing external conditions are so negative that, success becomes impossible under rational behaviour, and thus their absolute performance comes out to be negative. This second case should not be a problem in an intellectually-advanced society, but within the realities of our day, it is definitely a problem in most societies as their weakening Social Intellect does not let the agent believe in a fair evaluation for himself.

In both cases mentioned above, it usually becomes clear way before the end of the current term that the politicians on duty will end their term unsuccessfully (i.e. with a negative absolute performance), and thus they do not stand much of a chance to win the next election. In such cases, unless their goodwill is strong enough to prefer self-sacrifice over defeat, these politicians may start to look for a performance booster in their time left until the end of the current term, accepting all the *excessive risks* associated with it, as they have nothing left to lose. One classic way of taking such excessive risks in politics is heavy borrowing followed by public spending in the short-term to make everybody temporarily happy, with the hope that the voters will concentrate only on the recent past and give them another chance in the coming election. And once they can get the chance to stay on duty for another term, they will start praying for good luck (including very positive changes in external conditions) to come and save them somehow. The trouble here is that, good luck is sometimes unaware of its invitation for duty and fails to come, in which case the society pays the price of all those risks through higher taxes and lower economic growth for many years in the future. Even worse, when the amount of risks taken are extreme, the coming generations who are not even represented in politics today, will have to share and pay the price as well. Therefore, such excessive risk taking to manipulate the performance in the short run is in fact equivalent to cheating against the society.

In worse cases, the situation becomes so dire that, the politicians on duty realize they have no chance to even manipulate their own performance through any kind of performance boosters and some rival will replace them for sure in the next election. When there is no hope left for the next term, and if their goodwill has depreciated significantly, the politicians may move to a higher level in cheating and resort to totally irrational excessive risk taking, usually called *leaving-poison-pills-behind* in the jargon, this time aimed to ruin the performance of their rivals taking the job in the next election, with the hope that their rivals' potential failure following the next election will be worse than their own and will pave the way for themselves in the elections after that. Such behaviour works best in societies where there are just two main political parties and the voters have no choice but to toggle the government of the state between the two, in spite of the fact that the politicians on both sides have proven themselves to be incapable. Unfortunately, in today's world many societies are stuck with such two party domination[8]. Needless to say, the society happens to pay for all such poison pill exchanges, and at times the cumulative harm of such poison pills may ruin the whole system in the long run.

As discussed before, if the society can rise its Social Intellect such that it attracts the right agents to politics and elects them for duty, and then evaluates their performance properly, then the chances of facing the cases that may lead to excessive risk taking can be minimised. And it will help tremendously if, in addition, *the society becomes intellectual enough to realize that it should not accept and reward any success based on any kind of excessive risk taking*, so that even if such cases come along once in a while, the politicians will not try to cheat through taking excessive risks.

And regarding the poison pills, a more fundamental weakness in the current democratic systems, namely the non-existence of real competition in politics in most societies, has to be handled properly. As this issue will be discussed in detail in Book Two of this series, for the time being let it suffice to say that the society should learn to demand real and fair competition in politics, so that there will always be many political choices -instead of only two-, invalidating the rationale of leaving poison pills in the system.

4.6   The Rise Of The Populists

The Unexpected Reverse Trend

Contrary to the common belief, the causation relation between the Social Intellect and the wealth of a society is not a strong one. *A rise in Social Intellect is not a granted development resulting from a rise in the wealth.* A society may rise its income level and thus wealth in time, but that does not necessarily mean that it is rising its Social Intellect. Actually, wealth can rise very fast within decades but Social Intellect rises much more slowly, if at all, as rising intellect is almost a cultural change. Thus, *a society may catch up with the income level of another one within a short time, but may still lag way behind the other's intellectual level for a long time to come.*

Even when Social Intellect is rising, the speed of its rise depends on many factors. For instance, if the rising wealth of the society is not widely distributed, then the chances of a better education for the next generation will not be widely distributed either, preventing any fast increase in the overall Social Intellect of the society. And if the society is initially an autocracy, even if wealth rises and even if it is somewhat distributed to attain some social support for the autocrat, still the education channels may be deliberately kept closed to prevent an undesired rise in Social Intellect which may in time turn into an opposition against the autocrat. Such cases of slower speeds of increase in Social Intellect are common in many developing (or recently developed) non-western societies.

A worse case, however, can be observed in the economically advanced western societies in the latest decades: *a society may keep its wealth and income level intact, or may even be increasing it, but that does not mean that the society is not losing Social Intellect.* As this critical observation is against the common understanding in the western societies, the weakening of their Social Intellect still stays unrealised, and that has already started to threaten the functioning and therefore the very existence of their social order.

In the light of the above observations of the changes in wealth and Social Intellect *within* societies, the relative changes of wealth and Social

Intellect *between* societies can be analysed. As discussed above, even if societies may come closer in economic terms, they may still be staying apart in terms of Social Intellect, and one way of facing this result can be the underperformance of the economically-catching-up societies in developing their Social Intellect. Indeed, an initial shallow analysis may argue that, although the eastern societies are catching up with the western ones in economic terms in the latest decades, their political systems are not evolving towards functioning democracies, and thus politically they are not coming closer to the western ones, due to the fact that the development of their Social Intellect is lagging behind their economic developments. This may be partially true, but, unfortunately, this is not the whole story.

First of all, the political systems of the western and eastern societies are not staying apart, but on the contrary, they are actually getting closer. However, they are getting closer in the wrong direction.

Thanks to their losing Social Intellect at tremendous speeds, in many of the economically advanced western societies, the political systems are dangerously shifting towards autocracies-within-democracies. And in that cynical sense, as the western political systems are shifting towards autocracies, they are getting closer to those of the east, and thus the political systems of the economically advanced and developing (or recently developed) societies are actually getting closer. Unfortunately, the meeting point is not the desired one.

Therefore, it may be the time to analyse what has been going wrong with the political systems in the economically advanced societies as they lose their Social Intellect.

How Mainstream Politicians Lost Credit

By the end of the 20th century, the wealth of many economically advanced western societies have risen to very high levels with respect to many other societies of the world. But the voters in these western societies still had expectations of a stellar *absolute performance* from their politicians in the coming decades. The politicians, who mostly represented the mainstream parties by then, had to divert from rationality, and in their desperate try to satisfy the expectations of their voters, made too many difficult-to-fulfil promises.

The *external conditions* beyond the control of the politicians, however, were getting more and more cloudy. Within these western societies, the too liberal policies of the previous decades have risen the concentration of economic power and decreased competition in both goods/services and labour markets, creating a chain of reactions that eventually increased economic inequality, which in turn started to harm the welfare[9] of these societies. Technological advancements enabled more and more automation in production lines, increasing efficiency on the one hand, but decreasing the demand for less-qualified labour on the other. Many major corporations in the western societies have lobbied their governments for more economic globalisation solely considering their own benefit, and got what they wanted. As a result of this mis-structured economic globalisation, which will be discussed in another book of this series, they became global corporations and skyrocketed their fortunes. However, reaching new markets and new consumers was just one of the reasons behind the rise of their fortunes. Another equally significant reason was the access to cheap labour, which practically meant transferring wealth from the less qualified labour in their own societies to the labour in the developing societies. This resulted in a very uneven distribution of the benefits of globalisation, where the main loser was the labour in the western societies. Free trade further fuelled the flow of wealth from the western societies to the developing ones, as the inequalities in between were huge beforehand and thus there were many similar quality but much cheaper products the other societies can export to the western societies, harming many businesses in the western ones. The emerging trade surpluses to the benefit of the other societies were channelled back to the financial markets of the western societies and financed the borrowing-enabled consumption in the western societies – which enabled the rising inequality within their society to stay unnoticed for a long time. And all these simultaneous major changes in the environment and the rising complexity resulting from them, has caused a weakening of Social Intellect in the western societies, which has proceeded in the dark for decades. This has prevented the realisation of what has really been going on around by the masses, and the music played until it blew up in 2008.

To cut the long story short, *all the structural problems within and between the societies that have been accumulating for decades, have surfaced within a short period of time in such a way that they have created a perfect storm.*

For each society, this outburst of accumulated structural problems necessitates a major change in its macro-policies and strategies, and even in the main structure of its economic and political systems. And implementing such a major change will require a re-balancing of its short-term versus the long-term interests, with the long-term taking priority, such that the short-term sacrifices the society has to make to protect its long-term interests (and welfare) are now much higher than ever before. This is a fact that is extremely difficult for any society to accept, especially while its Social Intellect is weakening.

When these societies have faced a decrease in welfare, accompanied by a realisation of the heavy burden they have incurred, they have naturally but somewhat unfairly blamed their current mainstream politicians. On the surface, these societies were partially right, as their current politicians' ability and goodwill had significant deficiencies. However, they were partially wrong, because, even if their current politicians were perfectly capable and goodwilled, against those accumulated structural problems there was not much they could have done – apart from somewhat slowing down the loss of welfare experienced by these societies. In the framework of Section 4.4, when the negative external conditions that have been accumulating for decades surface undeniably, they can not be solved by any political agent within a couple of years, and a negative absolute performance in the short-term is inescapable.

It is unfortunate that due to the inadequacy of their Social Intellect these societies still fail to make a rational analysis, but rather prefer to open their minds to populism. However, it is not unexpected, simply because, if these societies had not been losing Social Intellect for decades, they would not have accumulated all these structural problems in the first place.

CREATING A BREEDING GROUND FOR THE POPULISTS

As discussed above, the shift from rationality to populism has not happened overnight. *The surfacing of the accumulated structural problems in both economics and politics over the latest decades, as a result of political mismanagement (i.e. the failure of the political agents), which in turn stems from the weakening of Social Intellect of the society (i.e. the failure of the principal), have eventually created a perfect breeding ground for the populists.*

Any social issue that needs deep analysis and painful long-term solutions, which makes it difficult to understand and painful to accept, is a candidate for the populist politician to feed on through mis-conceptions, wrong and shallow analysis, and irrational short-term solutions. And the more the society loses its Social Intellect, the easier it gets for the populist politician to misguide and persuade many voters. Thus came the rise of populism in the recent decades: very many accumulated structural troubles simultaneously surfacing on the one hand, society losing intellect further on the other. The perfect recipe for the perfect storm.

And indeed, many societies got so shocked and panicked that they have started to believe in populist promises. Interestingly enough, many of those populist politicians have promised to annihilate the Cheating Elite in economics (corporations and/or individuals), while themselves are trying to become the Cheating Elite in politics. And some societies have somehow believed in that.

EXTENDING UNDESERVED CREDIT TO POPULISTS

It may be tempting to believe that, a populist's coming to power may not be a problem in a democracy: even if a populist politician manages to win an election, once in power he will start to fail immediately. He either can not apply the promised policies since they are inapplicable in practise anyway, or applies some and the voters then experience the catastrophic results. Both ways will lead to a loss for him in the next election, and thus the problem will solve itself.

Wishfully thinking, there may be a bit of truth in this. However, even if this will be the case, a severe damage will already be done by the time the populist leaves power. *The populist not only worsens the existing problems by not treating them, but also adds new problems to the agenda by his painfully wrong policies. And this will steal decades from the future of the society and from the lives of the coming generations.*

To make matters worse, the damage done by the populist will depend on the time he will be allowed by the society to run the social system. In case a populist was elected just by a judgement mistake by the society, following a not-so-bad predecessor, his mistakes would not be tolerated for long by the society and thus his time in power would be limited to one term at best. However, *in the case of our day, the populist politician, if elected, will be coming after a series of mainstream politicians who performed terribly one after the other. Under this circumstance, the society will unfortunately extend further credit to the populist who promised radical changes, and will probably bear with him for longer. And a longer time in power means more damage to the system* – even to the point of total destruction. Therefore, the danger on the political horizon may be worse than initially thought.

Populists & The Fear Factor

The economic and political environment is getting ever more complex and changing ever faster for every society. As a result of this, on the one hand, new types of risks emerge naturally and frequently, and on the other hand, the society starts to lose Social Intellect and thus faces difficulty in deciding what and who to believe in.

Populist politicians merge these two developments. First they choose some convenient risks, exaggerate them heavily and promote them to existential level for the society – creating an artificial sense of insecurity and fear in the society. Then they present these issues as the only source of concern for the society's future, pushing aside or disqualifying all other major issues that are actually much more important than the chosen one – as another efficient way of distracting attention. Finally, they present themselves as the one and only saviour to solve that issue and save the society. And they usually present a set of solutions that are either imaginary (as in most cases the issue itself is rather imaginary) or inapplicable in practise (in the few cases where the issue has a touch of reality). If they can attract a large enough crowd of intellectually-children, they will start to have a say in politics or in time be elected to higher ranks (even all the way to the top) in legislative or executive bodies.

For the sake of being fair, it has to be confessed that not all the populists are born populists. Some politicians who were elected for other relatively more rational reasons initially, as they fail to deliver their promises under complex and/or negative external conditions, and as the society mis-evaluates their performance rather harshly, may shift to such populism to stay in power.

One way or another, most populist politicians are aware that their policies are doomed to fail eventually. Therefore, contrary to their initial promises, sooner or later, they start to look for alliances. Being the Cheaters in politics themselves, populist politicians usually and easily cooperate with other Cheaters in economics / markets, to promote their own collective interest at the expense of the society. And at the heart of their interests is the continuation of the political power which enables all of them to pursue their own agendas. And that usually requires moving further to extremes in time to strengthen their ties with the intellectually-childish voters who follow them.

Nationalism – Harms And Potential Benefits

Presenting issues of fear that commonly require a rise in nationalism to protect the society is the most common approach in populism in the recent decades. This is understandable as many populists find it easy and convenient to put the blame on the rise of globalisation during the recent decades - as it has become obvious after 2008 that globalisation in that form really had some very negative initially-hidden effects, one way or another on all societies including the economically advanced ones. And even more conveniently, the other-side in this equation (a collection of some other societies) practically can not defend themselves on the domestic political arena. Thus, nationalism emerged to be the most preferred way of populism in the recent decades.

Unfortunately, giving up on globalisation completely is harmful for the wealth and welfare of all societies both in the short-term and in the long-term as it degrades economic and political integration. However, a step-back in the short-term may also be a blessing in disguise for the long-term, as it may force looking for a change in the way globalisation works and enable globalisation to take some mutually beneficial form for all the participating societies and their members, instead of the mis-structured globalisation of the recent decades that brought major hidden harm to the global society, in addition to its widely advertised advantages. These issues of extreme importance will be addressed in detail in the coming books of this series.

The Real Existential Threats

When populists create artificial existential threats through exaggeration of practically minimal or moderate risks, they actually do a further major harm to the society, as they cause the real existential threats to stay beyond the social awareness and thus out of the current agenda of the society.

Some of those threats may be sorts of internal issues that can be and thus have to be handled within a society. However, many existential issues are global in the sense that no society can handle and fix them alone unless other societies co-operate.

One such issue is global warming, where unless all societies come to a common understanding and start applying the vital precautions in time, the problem will pass the point of no return and become a self-feeding one, after which chances of survival are minimal even if all carbon emissions are magically ceased overnight.

Another such threat is a major nuclear war that may materialize either deliberately or even incidentally. As the famous saying goes, nobody knows whether there will be such a third world war, but everybody can be sure that there will not be a fourth one.

The subject of this book, *the ongoing loss of Social Intellect in societies, is another sinister but persistent threat that feeds on itself, which may eventually make most societies practically ungovernable through democracies.* Although this may seem to be an internal problem for each society, actually it is a very global problem as every society is effected by the major developments in other societies in the integrated world of our day.

The first step to be taken to solve such global existential threats, is to realize that the societies of our day, and therefore their destinies, are much more integrated than ever before. This is simply because of the fact that such integration arises out of technological developments that are not reversible, and therefore trying to dis-integrate through weakening economic and political ties between societies will be of no practical effect.

Global cooperation is therefore the only solution. Unfortunately, it requires the existence of some basic Social Intellect at the society level for most societies, which is at best questionable for the time being. And to make matters worse, the rising trend of nationalism in many societies makes handling of global issues even more difficult than it used to be in the past.

The issues regarding global integration will be discussed in another book in this series, so for now it may suffice to remind that if the global society fails to solve even one of the existential threats it faces, which are not limited to those mentioned above, it will not need to worry on the rest. Therefore, it is a necessity to immediately start to tackle the core cause of all troubles, namely the lack of adequate Social Intellect in all societies. Unfortunately, rather than rising their current intellectual level, societies are currently busy with losing more of it.

Misery Of The Younger Generations

At every society the younger generations[10] are more competent at using the advanced communication channels that the latest technological developments have created and therefore they can keep up with the latest developments in economics and politics much easier and better. This enables the younger generations to somewhat compensate for their lack of adequate social education through gaining social experience faster. As a result the younger generations are losing Social Intellect much slower than the older generations. Or reading backwards, the older generations are losing Social Intellect much faster than the younger ones.

This creates a further problem in ageing societies, as older generations dominate their population and thus dominate the overall voting power and thus shape the political preferences of the society and the strongest policy demands. Therefore, as the effects of weakening Social Intellect are reflected heavily on the political system, the younger generations rightfully start to lose faith in democracy, as they can see much better that something is going very wrong with the political system.

To make matters worse, *although the younger generations have superior social experience on the developments of the recent past, they do not have a long-enough social memory that covers the events and developments of the distant past.* And as they lack the social experience on the events of the distant past, their realisation of the real value of democracy is also limited.

Thus emerges the dangerous combination: On the one hand, the younger generations see that democracy is functioning worse and worse every passing day. On the other hand, they lack the adequate social memory to value the virtues of democracy properly. Therefore, they may easily look for the wrong solution, namely, giving up on democracy too early and unnecessarily, and trying to replace it with some other vague political system advertised by the populists.

The Fall Of Democracy ?

The loss of Social Intellect gradually increases the difficulty of governing societies through a democratic system. At the initial stages, this may cause the rise of the populists. Populists in time may turn into extremists. In time, extremists may turn the political system into an autocracy-in-disguise. And eventually both the economic and political systems may break down and the society may face total chaos. And as the famous British philosopher Thomas Hobbes has argued centuries ago, the worst condition for a society is to be in chaos, and thus societies will even accept to have an autocratic leader than to stay in chaos.

The crucial observation that has to be made before it is too late is that, *even in a society currently governed by a functioning democracy, what starts as a loss of Social Intellect, in time may develop into a major existential threat for the political system such that the society may end up finding itself under an explicit autocracy.*

Therefore, preventing the loss of Social Intellect at the very beginning is the least costly option for the society, even though it requires a major reallocation of time, effort and resources to social education than ever done before. But this will at least keep democracy live and functioning.

Moreover, if the society can prevent the weakening of its Social Intellect in time, handling change and complexity will be managed much better through the democratic system, and thus the rise of fear of change and sense of insecurity can be prevented to a great extent. Prevention of the emergence of a wide group of intellectually-children who may fall prey to populism will then make it very difficult for the populist politician to promote manageable risks into existential fears for the society. There is no other real precaution to prevent the dominance of politics by populists and the ignition of the undesired chain reaction described above.

Finally, it has to be noted that, the prevention of the fall in the Social Intellect of the society is just the first step that needs to be taken to handle the ever rising complexity of the world. As the next step, major structural changes have to be made in the democratic system to enable it to handle the management of these changes adequately. Some of these necessary changes will be discussed in the final chapter, and the rest in another book of this series.

Chapter 5 : HIGH-TECH MEETS DEMOCRACY

5.1   Loss Of Faith In Expertise On Social Sciences

COMPLEX VERSUS RANDOM

As technology advances and   the societies get more integrated and therefore the economic and political environment gets more complex, new causations and new relevant variables that need not be considered before in social sciences enter the picture, and the lives of the academicians and the experts get tougher.

Analysing and understanding the general dynamics of social interactions is only the first stage in social sciences. The next and more important stage is forecasting the potential results of various policies accurately and thus guiding the society in the right direction to protect and promote its best interests. It is at this second stage that life gets exponentially complicated.

To start with, there is the difficult-to-forecast human variable, who may sometimes seem to act in mysterious ways. To complicate matters further, in the latest decades, due to the free flow of labour and immigration on the one hand, and exchanging views and opinions through advanced communication technologies on the other, distinct cultures have been integrating with each other within most societies. This is increasing the heterogeneity within the societies, and in line with that, the variety of human behaviour is also increasing.

In social interactions, in addition to the inherent difficulties in analysing the ever-changing causations and new variables, there are the so-called Butterfly Effects (a current minor development creating a major outcome in the long run through a yet-unforecastable chain of reactions) and Black Swans (the occurrence of very low probability but very high impact events) that can ruin the forecasts. And as the world gets more complex, more and more Butterflies and Swans start to fly around in economics and politics.

The rising heterogeneity in a society, coupled with the rising complexity in social interactions (within and between societies), make it ever more difficult to clarify the relations between the applied policies and their eventual outcomes. And when something gets too complex to understand, forecast and control, societies tend to consider it random. And considering them to be random feels better than confessing that the Social Intellect of the society can not cope with the speed of development around it and therefore is falling in relative terms.

Fortunately, being complex has nothing to do with being random. If economic and political developments were random, they could not be analysed, forecasted or controlled through various policies, which would make developing expertise impossible. However, as these developments are complex but not random, developing expertise is possible and will add tremendous value to the welfare of the society.

THE MISERY OF THE EXPERTS

When societies fail to understand the world around them, they are supposed to turn to the experts. But as the world gets too complex too fast, the relative ability of the experts in understanding and explaining whatever is going on, and in developing policies for the best interest of the society, suddenly falls. As a result, the experts on social sciences start to fail more frequently and more miserably in their analyses, forecasts and guidance.

Although the experts still have a much better chance of getting things right at every stage compared to the non-experts, when their success ratio falls the difference between the experts and the non-experts seem to disappear as the society has trouble in keeping the right statistics. And that arises the unfortunate doubt on whether expertise adds any value anymore in social sciences.

It is true that, even at times of less frequent and moderate developments, even the best of experts can not know what is definitely right (and thus is the best choice) in social sciences. However, even at times of rising complexity, they can still know what is definitely wrong, thus eliminating some courses of action and increasing the chances of making a better choice. And this fact alone is tremendously important, as any major policy mistakes will have significant costs for the society in the long run and thus avoiding them is vital, while, failing to choose the best option and going with the second or third best options will just have a conceptual opportunity cost for the long run and thus can be compensated on the way.

To illustrate, assume that there are 10 boxes of different shapes and colours, with gold in only one of them and the rest are empty. A random guess by a non-expert will have a chance of 1 out of 10 (10%) to find the gold. But if an expert knows that gold can not be in the blue or rectangular boxes, many boxes may get eliminated and the choices may decrease to say 2. Although it is still not known where the gold exactly is, it is at least known where it is not. Thus, chances of finding gold now improve to 1 out of 2 (50%).

Now assume that the world got more complex, such that the experts can only manage to decrease the number of choices to 3, which means that chances of finding gold is now 1 out of 3 (33%). The crucial observation here is that, although the success ratio of the experts has now decreased from 50% to 33%, it is still way above the success ratio of a non-expert which is still just 10%. Therefore, although the success ratio of the experts fell, it still makes perfect sense to listen to the experts rather than making a non-expert bet.

The example can be further complicated by assuming that, in addition to the one box containing gold, two other boxes now have a poisonous gas in them. A random guess by a non-expert will now have a chance of 2 out of 10 (20%) to open a poisonous box and end up dead. Now, if the experts can eliminate the ones with the poisonous gas, and decrease the options as above, not only the chance of finding gold is higher with respect to the non-expert bet, but more importantly, the risk of opening a box with poisonous gas -with fatal consequences- is totally avoided. Finding the gold in the second or third trial rather than the first one will mean spending some extra time and effort, but is still acceptable, while opening a box with poisonous gas and ending up dead is an irreversible catastrophe.

It can therefore be concluded that, *even at times when too many major developments occur too frequently and thus expertise falls relatively, seeking expert advice still adds value to the welfare of the society. But more importantly, seeking expert advice significantly decreases the risks of facing catastrophic outcomes that may result in a system breakdown. Therefore, when the complexity of the world rises exponentially, as it has been happening in recent decades, the society needs to listen to the experts even more, rather than less, as avoiding wrong choices and thus a system breakdown must be the priority at times of trouble. This is simply because missing the best course of action can always be compensated as long as the system survives, but if the system collapses a recovery will be extremely difficult.*

THE SINS OF THE EXPERTS

The fall in the ability and thus the success rate of the experts as the complexity of the world rises, is a reality that can neither be denied nor be avoided. The society should learn to live with that.

A second and worse problem, which is avoidable and thus not acceptable, is the fall in the goodwill of the experts. The spreading phenomenon of expertise-for-sale to concentrated interest groups, including the Cheaters, in the sense that the expert opinion presented to the society is misguiding or only reflects some parts of truth that are preferred by the concentrated interest groups and omits some of the non-preferred but vital facts, creates a loss of trust in the experts. *Once cases of such tailor-made misguiding opinions start to spread, society naturally loses faith in the goodwill of the experts, making their ability irrelevant. This results in a self-destruction of the value of expertise at a time when it is needed most.*

5.2   The Human Variable

The human variable is naturally at the heart of the design of the economic and political systems and the analysis and setting of various social policies. Unfortunately, the complexity of the human nature makes such analysis extremely complicated.

To illustrate, consider a simple question on human nature: Given two options, one good and one bad, which one will an individual choose?

The classic naïve answer would be the good one, which unfortunately does not reflect the reality. A more mature, but still simple answer, would be sometimes the good and sometimes the bad one. And although this is closer to reality, it still does not help to make any analysis or derive any conclusions.

A more advanced rational answer will be based on the intellectual level of the individual. If the intellectual level of the individual is high, he will make a conscious choice and most probably choose the good one, although, with a lower probability, he may still prefer to choose the bad one. If the intellectual level of the individual is low, he simply will not be able to distinguish the good from the bad, and thus his choice will be a random one, meaning that half of the times he will choose the good, and half of the times the bad. This answer may still seem to be vague on an individual basis, as there is no definite choice in any case. However, when the society at large is considered, statistics will play its part to enable us to reach significant conclusions: in a society where the intellectual level of individuals is high, the choice of good will dominate the choice of bad, thus enabling the society to end up at the good choice. However, in a society where the intellectual level of individuals is relatively low, the choices of good and bad will balance each other and thus where the society ends up becomes a random event. Indeed, many valuable academicians has demonstrated the existence of such randomness in societies' destinies in their relevant historical studies[11].

Considering the effect of the average intellectual level of societies in determining their destinies, and confessing that a society with a high intellectual level was historically non-existent, there is no way to disagree with these academicians regarding such randomness in the past. However, if one day a society with a high intellectual level comes into existence, as with the latest communication technologies it may now be possible, its destiny will not be a random event. Just on the contrary, it can be argued that, when the intellectual level of the society rises beyond a certain threshold, its chances of reaching the good end also rise significantly. But now the analysis is more complicated as it introduced the further dimension of intellect. However, both the analysis and the conclusion look more rational and useful now, as now they define a clear policy target, namely rising the Social Intellect of the society.

Unfortunately, neither the analysis, nor the conclusion is complete yet.

There is also a so-called behavioural answer. It says that, given the choice between the good and the bad, the individual with a low intellectual level, who can not differentiate the good and the bad anyway, will simply choose the *easy* one[12]. Thus, the analysis regarding a society where the intellectual level of individuals are relatively low changes: the end result will not be a random event at all, but depends on which choice is easier, or deliberately made easier by some others. Now both the analysis and the conclusion are further complicated, as another additional dimension regarding the easiness of the choices is introduced, but they are closer to reality. And still, the analysis is not complete.

A further dimension that needs to be taken into consideration is the existence of the Cheaters, namely those with a high intellectual level but with a preference for the bad choice in the sense that they choose to promote their own interests through harming those of the society. They will try and most probably succeed to manipulate the opinion of the intellectually-children in the society in both economics and politics, through false promises covering easy benefits or solutions, such that the intellectually-children will behave in a way that will benefit the Cheaters and harm themselves. And now there is almost no randomness left, and the analysis came closest to the reality of our day.

THE NECESSARY UPGRADE IN THE ANALYSIS OF HUMAN BEHAVIOUR

The human variable and its analysis are always complex.

Historical analysis techniques were based on the assumption that, individuals mostly behave rationally, and even though they may sometimes behave irrationally such diversions from rationality on an individual basis will cancel out each others' effects, resulting in an overall rational behaviour for the society. In the distant past, such analysis might have been satisfactory. But not anymore.

It can be guessed from the discussion above that, now a proper analysis has to be based on the Social Intellect dimension of the human variable. However, Social Intellect is not a concept of black and white clarity. Just on the contrary, there are infinitely many shades of grey in between when considered on an individual basis. And to make matters worse, the intellectual level of each individual is continuously changing over time.

If the changes in Social Intellect on an individual basis were random, that is to say if the Social Intellect of one individual was rising while that of another was falling, then their net effect on the society basis might have been minimal. However, as the complexity of the world is rising for everybody, almost all individuals are simultaneously losing Social Intellect, albeit at different rates. Therefore, there will be no cancelling out, but a net falling trend in the Social Intellect of the society.

In principle, a proper analysis should take Social Intellect as a primary input, but unfortunately, it is difficult to carry out such analysis in practice with the classic analytical and statistical tools. This is due to the fact that it is practically impossible to track and analyse each individual separately and continuously, and therefore, in the lack of such surveillance capability it is difficult to assess the overall Social Intellect level of the society at any given point in time.

And to complicate matters further, there are the manipulative efforts of the Cheaters. As the potential effectiveness of manipulation on an individual basis depends both on the Social Intellect level of the individual and the ability of the manipulator, both of which are changing over time, analysing the net effect of manipulation by classic statistical tools is also difficult.

Reading backwards, if it becomes possible (a) to track the behaviour of each individual very closely and continuously on a personal basis, enabling an accurate assessment of his current Social Intellect, (b) to measure the effectiveness of any manipulation effort on an individual basis, and (c) to have the computing power to aggregate huge amounts of data to drive a meaningful conclusion on a society basis, then a very accurate analysis can be made. Furthermore, such capacity will pave the way for developing much stronger manipulation methods.

And then, everything will change.

5.3   Alone Against Artificial Intelligence

High Tech Monopolies On Data & Information Flow

During the recent decades, following the technological advancements in digital communications, emerging high-tech companies operating on digital networks introduced the strange case of offering their valuable services to all users free of any financial charges. And that was something that no society was conceptually prepared for, especially after decades of exposure to practical education on the virtue of getting financial rewards for any contribution to the society. This conceptually new approach caught everybody off guard.

Years after the emergence of these high-tech companies, the societies understood that these companies charge them in terms of a new currency, namely information. And to make matters worse, these high-tech companies became monopolies before the societies could realize what was really happening. Then a new story began to unfold.

On the one hand, these high-tech companies have access to all the personal information on their users, including their economic and political preferences and behaviour, which turn into a valuable asset once analysed through many advanced algorithms. And when such companies can operate as monopolies in their respective fields, they have practical access to the personal information on an individual basis for almost all the members of the society, as there is practically no alternative platform any individual can get such service. So no one can escape their data base. And then their so-called big-data algorithms that run on this society-wide data can reveal causations and correlations[13] clearly, and *this enables the accurate prediction of the behaviour of both the individuals and the society under various conditions*. Therefore, their infinite access to such personal information enables these companies to know their users even better than the users know themselves.

On the other hand, they control the flow of data to their users. And when such companies can operate as monopolies in their respective fields, their users have no other source to double-check any information they are allowed or not allowed to get. Therefore, such high-tech monopolies may potentially direct the information flow to their own interests, or to the interests of those they may be cooperating with. *They can potentially wipe out any person, any corporate or political entity, or any idea that they don't want their users to get informed on. Even worse, they can generate fake information promoting any person, any corporate or political entity, or any idea and mis-guide the society* [14].

Finally, when the capability to have personal information and analysis for each individual in the society, combines with the capability to control information flow on an individual basis, a tremendous power emerges. With such power, the manipulation of the opinion and the perception of every individual and thus the society, on every imaginable dimension spanning from economics to politics, becomes possible.

At the most innocent cases, such power can be utilized to generate economic profits, while at more dangerous cases it can be used to manipulate political choices. And *once the society loses its ability to freely access correct and complete information, there will be perfect information asymmetry which may eventually result in total system failure in both economics and politics.*

Digital Media And The Birth Of A Wrong Perception Of Equality

The previous section discussed how the technological developments gave birth to high-tech monopolies and the colossal manipulative power they have accumulated in just a few decades. The well known reason that enabled the easy formation of such monopolies is the nature of the networking-function on which most of them base their services – everything works best when everybody is on the same network. However, their manipulative power does not only stem from their monopoly status. The equally important but much less recognized fact is that, during the same couple of decades, the societies were losing Social Intellect at a tremendous pace.

This loss of Social Intellect of the society poured fuel to the fire in two separate ways. First, it caused the society to mis-judge and mis-use the new technological capabilities offered to them, and fall prey to its own misunderstanding. Second and worse, it practically made the society more vulnerable to manipulation in case these monopolies develop such intentions.

THE BLESSING AND THE CURSE

Thanks to the ever advancing communication technologies, societies now have widespread easy access to endless information, which, in principle, must be beneficial in supporting the Social Intellect of all societies. In less intellectual societies where information used to be a very scarce resource, the sudden spread of information may indeed help rising Social Intellect. And in more intellectual societies it may at least slow down the loss of Social Intellect.

Advanced communication technologies also enabled individuals to freely express their opinion, which initially seemed to be a blessing for the intellectual development of the societies and therefore for democracy.

Unfortunately, the practise came out to be somewhat different than expected.

BOOSTED EGOS

One main reason why people love digital media so much is that it offers complete freedom and absolute equality in utilizing it: an individual can read (or access information on) anything and speak on (or supply information on) anything as he wishes. This freedom and equality in commenting on anything, creates an implicit ego boosting for individuals, making them believe that having the means to comment on anything gives them the natural right to comment on anything, regardless of whether they have any background education, relevant experience or necessary information that will enable them to make comments which may create value for anybody else, let alone the society. Thus, the spread of digital media willingly or unwillingly introduced an everybody-knows-and-can-express-an-opinion-on-everything state of mind, a major fallacy for the society.

FEELING NO NEED TO IMPROVE ONESELF OR LISTEN TO EXPERT OPINION

When digital media gives an individual the means to comment on anything, it also makes him feel qualified to do so, which in turn makes him believe that he need not search and respect expert opinion and learn from them, practically meaning that he will not bother to spare time and effort to increase his intellectual level. And, from a political viewpoint, this is exactly what the Cheating Elite are praying for: when one is unaware of his weaknesses, he is manipulated, played and fooled easily, towards serving the interests of the Cheating Elite, with terrible consequences for the welfare of the society and democracy.

BEING CLOSED TO CONTRADICTORY OPINION

Individuals have a tendency to easily believe in arguments they like, namely those supporting their own opinions and desires, without demanding much of a solid proof or deep analysis. On the contrary, when faced with arguments they do not like, namely those that are contradictory to their own opinions or desires, they demand a zillion undeniable proofs and analysis. In most cases, it is practically impossible to make an individual even to listen to (let alone accept) contradictory opinions without disproving and invalidating his existing ones first. Thus, expecting an individual to change his opinion all by himself, through searching and listening to contradictory opinions by himself, is already a weak bet. This may only be done by the intellectually-adults, who, unfortunately, make up only a small proportion of each society.

The digital media serves to make this already difficult process totally impossible, by enabling an individual to look for and easily find people who think like him and opinions that support those of his own. Therefore, the freedom and capability to reach other opinions through the digital media, to face contradictory ones and thus improve one's own intellectual level in principle, rather serves the opposite in practise, by enabling an individual to find and cluster with those who think like himself, making him an even firmer believer of his own opinion, even if it is totally nonsense. And in cases where the individual may fail to reach the supporters of his own opinions, the algorithms embedded in digital media platforms will do the job for him.

No platform bothers to use algorithms that find and bring contradictory opinions to those of an individual. These platforms' natural aim, from an economic perspective, as the excuse goes, is to maximise the happiness of their users in utilizing these platforms. And this conveniently transforms to maximising the users' addiction to these platforms, and thus maximising their indirect revenues by maximising the number of their addicts, without having any economic reason to try to aid the intellectual development of the addicts. Makes perfect economic sense. And so the society accepts, and so the Cheating Elite gladly know.

NO PLACE FOR INTELLECTUAL COMMUNICATION

Thanks to the digital media platforms, now everybody can read anything and speak on anything as he wishes. Though this seems to elevate the free flow of information to never before reached heights, the trouble is that, people mostly read little and speak a lot, while just the opposite had to happen for digital media to make a positive contribution to the intellectual development of the society. When so many speak and so few listens, the media gets filled with monologues, with little capacity left for dialogues which are the real drivers of sensible communication and thus rise the intellectual level of individuals.

CENSORSHIP THROUGH NOISE

Freedom of speech, in the sense of freedom of expression, is of no use to the society if all an individual can hear is unqualified junk opinion. *Freedom of speech creates value only when it enables qualified opinions on contradicting sides to reach the whole society, and let the society listen and judge which side is right.* When so many people -most of whom are totally unqualified to comment on the relevant issue- talk simultaneously, all an individual can hear is noise and garbage that do not add value to his intellectual development, but instead just steal away his time and attention from other potentially value creating activities. Thus, when functioning this way, the digital media becomes a so-called lemons market where the unqualified noise distracts any qualified ones.

Therefore, *what initially seemed to be a perfect environment for freedom of speech, practically ended up censoring out many expert opinions that the society actually needs to hear* [15], *as the very many participants in the digital media self-appointed as experts, accompanied by some fake or ill-willed experts deliberately created or fed by the Cheating Elite, shout in unison to crowd out those with real expertise and goodwill.*

JUST WHEN THE SOCIETY NEEDS EXPERTS

All the undesired side effects of the digital media mentioned above actually stem from the fact that the society is missing the intellectual level required to properly handle the new capabilities offered by the digital media. And that is no surprise as the society is losing Social Intellect within a world that is getting ever more complex day by day. However, this is exactly when the society needs the guidance of the experts most. Unfortunately, an environment where the opinions of the experts and the non-experts get mixed up without distinction undermines the trust in both the ability and the goodwill of the experts, and brings more harm than good to the society.

Artificial Intelligence And Manipulation Through Controlling Flow Of Information

The exponential rise in computing power in the recent years make it possible to follow every breath that every individual takes in the digital environment. When the digital footprint of each individual on different networks can be tracked and analysed in detail, it becomes possible to know the individual better than he knows himself and to predict his behaviour and expected reactions with almost perfect accuracy. And then, as the next step, his decisions and actions can be manipulated as well.

And then the analysis made on an individual basis can be aggregated utilizing big data algorithms, to drive meaningful conclusions on the society basis. And once the society's expected reactions can be predicted, it becomes possible to manipulate the society's decisions and behaviour as well. All that is needed then is the control of flow of information.

A MAJOR CHANGE IN THE GAME

The revolutionary change enabled by the statistical analysis based on high-tech surveillance and computing capabilities is that, it can predict and manipulate how the individual behaves, without the need to understand why the individual behaves (or will behave) that way. And the same is valid for the society. Prediction and manipulation based on such capabilities do not need to make any complicated causation analysis, and thus do not necessitate any expertise on social sciences either, *making this new tool of manipulation the easiest to be used by concentrated interest groups and therefore the most dangerous.*

CONTROLLING THE FLOW OF INFORMATION

If some concentrated interest groups, namely the Cheating Elite[16], can control the flow of information such that they can decide the information that will and will not reach each individual, they will have the power to manipulate both his economic and political opinions, and misguide him to act for their benefit rather than for his own. And the successful manipulation of most of the individuals will practically result in the manipulation of the society.

Manipulation, however, still requires fine tuning.

From one perspective, any manipulator has to control the flow of information in two dimensions. First, he should control the flow of *society-wide information* to which everybody has access to, and second, he should control the flow of *custom-tailored information* to which only the individual will be exposed to on a personal basis.

From another perspective, the manipulator should make sure that any *information against his interests* should not reach either to the individual or to the society, and any *manipulative information that suits his own interests* should reach to the individual, and in some cases to the society.

The first part, namely preventing the spread of information against the manipulator's interests, can be done in many ways. One way is controlling the search engines that will do the censorship for the manipulator without being known by the society. Another way, which is more effective, is to crowd out the environment with too much noise that any undesired information will not be noticed by the society. And thanks to the recent developments in artificial intelligence, creating noise on a grand scale is now much simpler.

The distribution of manipulative information, however, requires more attention.

FABRICATING MISINFORMATION

As discussed in Section 4.6, in the political arena of the latest decade, the populists managed to persuade so many people so effectively in a short time without even utilising much of an artificial intelligence, and many societies witnessed the emergence of autocracies-hiding-behind-democracies. Now imagine what can happen once the populists start to use the capabilities of artificial intelligence.

On the one hand, artificial intelligence makes the production of fake photos, audio recordings, videos, stories, news and all other sorts of digital material so easy. On the other hand, in both macro-economics and politics, populist stories with easier and faster solutions are naturally more effective than telling the true solutions that usually requires making short term sacrifices while waiting for long-term results. Therefore, by the nature of the deal, the capabilities introduced by artificial intelligence will benefit the populist manipulator much more than the rational goodwilled expert. And, as discussed before, all gets worse when the society's Social Intellect weakens in the meantime.

THE TRICK OF THE TRADE

The development of artificial intelligence enables easy fabrication of manipulative information. The spreading of fabricated information, however, is trickier. Any fabricated information that will serve the interests of a specific manipulator at the expense of the society, but without harming those of any other concentrated interest group, can be fed through society-wide channels, without getting much counter reaction from anybody and thus without being invalidated immediately. And this is usually the case in micro-economic matters. However, in spreading any manipulative information that will hurt another concentrated interest group, as in all political issues where an opposition is constantly on the watch, using society-wide channels is not a highly effective option, as the opposition will most probably not let the misinformation survive for too long without a counter reaction. Political manipulation, therefore, becomes tremendously more effective when done through personal communication channels.

CUSTOM TAILORED CONTROL OF INFORMATION FLOW ON AN INDIVIDUAL BASIS

The latest developments in the communication technology enables the digital media and networks to control the flow of information on an individual basis. On top of that, the developments in artificial intelligence enables the *tailor-made production* of manipulative and/or fake photos, videos, stories, news and all other sorts of digital material, *based on each individual's personal digital footprint.*

As each individual's digital footprint reveals his personal background, beliefs, preferences, tendencies, desires and especially intellectual weaknesses, *such personal production of manipulative material will have maximum effect on shaping his perception and opinion on every imaginable dimension including economics and politics*, and will definitely make him a much easier prey for manipulation.

To make matters worse, even though in the digital world each individual has zillions of contacts, in the physical world he is getting ever lonelier. He now has fewer friends whom he can trust through shared and tested past experience and intimate personal history. Instead, he is submerged in an artificial environment in the virtual digital world, where most of the times the algorithms guide (read: decide) whom he should contact with or follow. At some point many individuals are left with no reliable reference to check out the reality anymore and become fully open to mis-guidance and manipulation.

The final nail on the coffin is that, when a manipulator gets control of such custom-tailored information production and flow, *the individual will be the only person receiving such fake or manipulative information, without anybody else knowing it. Therefore, nobody else will have a chance to counter-argue against that manipulative information or reveal its invalidity.* Any such fabricated information will then stay unopposed and thus will be taken to be correct by the receiving individual.

It is even possible that, through such personalization of fabricated information contradictory messages can be sent to different individuals. From a political viewpoint, a manipulator may promise some individuals to increase something, while promising to other individuals to decrease the same thing, taking the political support of both simultaneously. As neither will know of the information sent to the other, none will realize that contradictory false promises are made.

The effectiveness of personally fabricated and personally sent manipulative information is higher for every individual, as the information hits the individual where he is most open to be influenced and stays unopposed. However, in relative terms, the intellectually-children are still more open to such manipulation, as their high (mis)perception of their own intellect makes them more vulnerable. From a political perspective, this means that, once the already polarised / extremist voter is exposed to such manipulation, he will be even more polarised, with little hope left to change his mind for the milder. Time, therefore, is running out to take precautions against the use of artificial intelligence for manipulative purposes.

The intellectually-adults will definitely be aware that they should not give much credit to manipulative information generated by artificial intelligence. However, in an environment where it is not possible to distinguish between the information generated by the manipulators versus the information coming from genuine good-willed experts, such awareness will practically result in censorship: the valuable and honest communication will be ignored together with the manipulative one. And such censorship of rational and/or opposing voices will still be a benefit for the concentrated interest groups trying to manipulate the society.

WHAT CAN BE DONE

The rising ability to control the fabrication and distribution of custom-tailored information flow will be a perfect weapon for all sorts of concentrated interest groups trying to manipulate the society.

Fortunately, the societies still have some time before such manipulative capacities reach perfection. One reason is that, artificial intelligence is still in development stage and has not reached its full potential power yet. And the other reason is that, the older generations, thanks to their marginal use of the latest technological developments, have only a vague footprint on digital environment. For the time being, this prevents the individual analysis, fabrication and distribution of information from becoming a society-wide phenomenon, thus preventing the manipulation of the whole society.

And this gives the society a chance to take some vital precautions before time runs out.

First, *the society should realize that any monopolies or any concentration of power in the digital environment, enabling information gathering, analysis, fabrication (through artificial intelligence) and flow on a society-wide scale is too dangerous and can potentially harm the interests of the society* and even the stability of the social order. The failure of both the regulators and the society in the recent past in recognizing these potential dangers of the existence of such monopolies has significantly increased the cost of dealing with these monopolies today. Considering the potential negative consequences, however, the society should be willing to pay the high price to break up such monopolies (and regulate artificial intelligence) before it is too late.

Custom-tailored information fabrication and flow on an individual basis can be extremely effective, especially in politics, because of the fact that the existence of such information can not be detected by anybody else apart from the targeted individual himself, and therefore it is impossible for any goodwilled experts (or the rivals of the manipulators) to oppose or invalidate the fabricated information. Therefore, a second way of guarding the individuals from such personally fabricated information is to increase their awareness, such that they will only believe in the information that is publicly available. This way, each individual can be sure that whatever he hears will be heard by everybody else, and whatever everybody else hear will be heard by himself, thus, any opposing or invalidating information will also be available through some other public resources in the right time and manner.

Finally, the third and the best way is creating new structures for reliable public sources of information and expertise, as will be discussed in Chapter 6.

Chapter 6 : HOW TO RISE SOCIAL INTELLECT

6.1   Social Education

Within the environment of our day, where too many things change too much too fast, no individual can get enough of Social Intellect through the natural pace of accumulating social experience in his daily life. On the contrary, leaving the learning process to its own devices will only result in a continuous loss of Social Intellect for the individual, and thus for the society. *Social Intellect can cope up with the stunning pace of developments only if there is a jump-start of social education to enable an initial catch-up with the way the world works, followed by a continuous care and effort to stay aware.*

Aim And Scope Of Social Education

To serve the desired purposes, social education must span the basics of the primary social sciences of politics, economics, finance, law and sociology. This will enable each individual to understand the dynamics of the economic and political systems of the society. Only after getting such a basic social education, followed by a real-life social experience, an individual can attain social awareness, and can be considered as an intellectually-adult. Otherwise, he will remain intellectually-childish for a lifetime, making him an easy prey for the Cheaters.

The aim of social education is not, and can not be, to create an economics or politics expert out of each individual. All that is required of social education is to make each member of the society intellectual enough to be able to understand and evaluate the analysis of the real experts in social sciences, so that he can attain and keep social awareness, and make rational choices as a consumer and a voter.

CREATING AN AUDIENCE FOR THE EXPERTS

Academicians and experts in economics and politics seem to have this strange habit of communicating only among themselves, with a cool but unnecessary jargon of their own, and show utmost care not to share their expertise, analyses and ideas with the public. This may partially be due to the fact that the probability of being misunderstood by the under-educated public is pretty high. Such potential misunderstanding may cause an unintentional misguidance creating more harm than good, or may even result in negative personal consequences for the experts. However, if widespread social education becomes the norm within the society, experts in social sciences may find the motivation and the means to communicate better with the public, feeding vital information and analysis to the society, increasing its social experience and keeping it aware of the latest developments. This will further increase the intellectual level of the society and let them make better economic and political choices, which will further motivate the real experts to share their opinion with the public, and so on. All that is needed, therefore, is to start the chain reaction sometime somewhere. And this can best be ignited by establishing a social education infrastructure for the society and thus creating an audience for the experts.

BUILDING AN INTELLECTUAL INFRASTRUCTURE

The first aim of social education must be teaching each individual how to think and analyse continuously, rather than presenting a set of information that he is supposed to believe in without questioning. And following that, *social education has to present all the major alternate and contradictory opinions regarding economic and political issues, as nobody has a definite correct answer to the relevant questions. In fact, the correct answer, even if there is one, definitely changes from society to society, and from time to time within each society.* Therefore, the aim of social education should be to present the basics of all the alternative major approaches to such issues, and *let the individual gain the ability to understand the analysis of experts at specific times and under specific conditions, to eventually make the final decision of his own.*

When the basic education system fails to establish this intellectual infrastructure, all those individuals who remain to be intellectually-children prefer to be only told what is the answer without feeling the need to know why that may be the answer, and then end up accepting misleading information easily and acting on it, eventually facing the negative consequences.

To sum up, social education has to build an intellectual infrastructure first, present the basics of social sciences next, and while doing so, clarify that learning is a lifelong process as everything that is discussed in some way at some time can and probably will change in the future.

Education As A Dangerous Weapon

History is full of great ideas eventually used for the wrong purposes. Unless social education is very delicately structured, it will easily be a strong candidate to become a manipulative tool that may do more harm than good to the society.

The aim of social education is to create intellectually-adults out of initially innocent individuals. In order to do that, it has to teach the very basics of social sciences so that each individual can understand and evaluate the developments he will face for a lifetime (with the help of the experts of the field) and make rational choices that serve his own interests. But to be able to accomplish that, *social education has to present all the major alternate opinions on the basic choices regarding the economic and political issues.*

Even on the macro concepts of social sciences, there are no undisputable right answers that are valid at all times and places, but there are alternate opinions regarding the best choices depending on the specific conditions. To illustrate, in economics, there are contradicting opinions on how free the market should be, how much regulation and state interference is appropriate, how strong and protective a social security system should be, how much taxation brings net benefits to the society, how much the economy should be opened to global flows, how should a crises be handled, whether monetary or fiscal policy has to be used, how much the next generation can be burdened by current actions, and many more. In politics, there are contradicting opinions, starting with whether democracy or autocracy is better, how much meritocracy should be integrated to the system, how liberal a democratic system should be, how should the separation of powers be within the system, how should the relation of the individual with the society be arranged, how should the national culture and values of the society be protected against global integration in many dimensions, and many more. Nobody has definite correct answers to any of these questions, and in fact, the correct answer, even if there is one, changes from society to society, and from time to time within each society. The aim of social education should be to present the basics of all the alternative major approaches to such issues, and let the individual gain the ability to understand the environment and the relevant analysis of experts at specific times and under specific conditions, and eventually make the final decision of his own.

If the social education agenda is fixed to present only one side of the alternative opinions, it will have absolutely no use in increasing the intellect of the individuals and the society. Instead, it will become a perfect tool for the manipulation of the innocent to the direction desired by whoever is controlling the preparation of the social education program. It may be used to emphasize only the virtues of the existing or some other system, and people may become more blind-sighted rather than more socially aware after taking the program. In our previous jargon, it may become a manipulation tool for the Cheaters, enabling them to hide some light grey options that will not serve their interests.

To illustrate, consider the existing education systems. Even at the university level many things that are taught as principles-not-needed-to-be-further-questioned are actually not the whole truth, or are sometimes simply false. Remember the bull story at Section 3.2, where on the surface there seems to be a competition between the matador and the bull, but actually the end result is already known from the beginning as the bull was *educated to lose*. The current economics education in the western societies is actually a similar case. On the one hand, the virtue of competition is thought to everyone either through formal education or through social expertise. On the other hand, it is conveniently forgotten to mention that competition creates value for the society if and only if it is fair. And the society is made to accept the validity of this half-truth without the right to have any doubt, such that even discussing the validity of the virtue of competition is considered to be a sign of ignorance or foolishness.

For that reason, many of those individuals who would have succeeded under fair competition but actually have lost because of the cheating of others, still naively believe that it was their own inadequateness (weakness, laziness, mistakes etc) that made them lose and there is nothing wrong with the functioning of the economic and political systems. Given no right to be suspicious of cheating, they show no political reaction, or at least under-react. And this way, *the ethical individuals are educated to lose in the competition.*

Sooner or later, when the society becomes aware of the widespread cheating in the system, something worse happens. Suddenly all the losers, including those who would have lost even under fair competition due to their own inadequacy, start to think that they have lost just because something is wrong with the economic and political systems. And then there will emerge a society-wide over-reaction, which at best will bring populists to the government, and at worst will destroy the whole social order and bring chaos to ruin everybody's lives for a long time.

Building A Social Education Program

The mere existence of a social education program will be of no use to the society, and worse, may even harm the society, unless the content of the program is designed to cover alternate opinions. The content of social education is therefore a matter of vital importance to the welfare of the society, and must be handled and determined accordingly. And this observation leads to two conclusions, both in principle and in practise.

The first is that, *getting a proper social education that covers all major alternate views regarding economic and political issues is a basic right of each member of the society.* It will not be an exaggeration to demand this basic right to be protected by the law, even by the Constitution.

The second is that, *in order to have complete and unbiased coverage, the preparation and running of the social education program must be the responsibility of some Independent Institution within the political system*, rather than the current Executive Authority (the government or the president). And in line with the same logic, the formation and functioning of this Independent Institution has to be under the supervision of the Legislative Authority within the political system (the parliament or equivalent). Finally, the contents and application of the program have to be approved by a *super-majority* (say, by 65%-75%) in the Legislative Authority in order to guarantee its objectivity.

Social education will add value to the welfare of the society if and only if these principles are adhered to. Otherwise it will just be a manipulative tool for whoever is controlling it and thus will harm the interests of the society.

SOCIAL EDUCATION MUST BE MANDATORY

There is a minimum threshold level, meaning a minimum coverage and a minimum duration, for any education program, before which it has no effect, and that level is not trivially low. Social education, even if proper, is not a magic medicine that can change the intellectual level of the society overnight with the slightest dose. It should accumulate over years, increasing from generation to generation, to be most effective. Therefore, it is in the best interest of the society to make sure that each and every member of the society gets a meaningful dose of social education so that the accumulation process can work.

In practise, this will mean that there should be a mandatory basic social education program, lasting for a full year at the minimum for the coming generations. Needless to say, from an individual's perspective a year is not a short period, but it is not as long as it used to be within the ever-lengthening lifespans either. Moreover, *getting a proper social education is not only a personal right, but also the responsibility and thus the duty of each individual to his society,* as increasing the intellectual level of the individual and the society is a matter of life or death for the well functioning and sustainability of the economic and political systems.

Historically, almost all societies accepted the need for a mandatory military training for their male members, during their most productive ages, usually lasting more than a year, simply because they all realized that such training is a matter of life or death for the society under potential conditions of military conflict with the other societies. In other words, societies accepted to spare huge time and resources in military training, to guard against the *mere probability* that there may be a case of conflict.

Therefore, all that is needed for the establishment of such a mandatory social education program is the realization by the society that improving its intellectual level is also a matter of life or death for the sustainability of its economic and political system - assuming a democracy. The crucial difference is that, in case the intellectual level of a society falls and lags behind the increase in the complexity of the environment, its system will *definitely* fail sooner or later.

Finally, just like military training being useless at an early age when individuals are not physically-adults yet, social education will also be useless before individuals become mentally-adults. Therefore, the appropriate time for taking the social education program must be after the ages 18-21, as most individuals practically start to develop an initial awareness of the political and economic environment only by then.

Social Education And The Cheaters

Rising Social Intellect is a nightmare for the Cheaters as it makes manipulation of the society much more difficult. And the first step in rising intellect is social education. Preventing or at least weakening social education will make sure that even if the individuals can reach adequate information and spare the required time and effort to evaluate it, their efforts will still be in vain. Although it is not practically possible for the Cheaters to prevent every member of the society from becoming intellectually-adult, it is enough to keep the majority intellectually-childish. And then, all that is needed is to prevent an effective communication between the two, and manipulate the intellectually-children as desired.

Thanks to the fast advancement in communication technologies during the latest decades, even without the existence of any social education programs, the free flow of information within and across the societies now started to tear down the walls of ignorance, and at least some individuals started to learn what they can and should rationally demand in both economics and politics. The utilisation of such information is not wide spread yet, making the rise in the intellectual levels of societies through such flow a slow process, but at least it is unstoppable. In other words, as a positive side effect of advanced communications, the Cheaters can not prevent the spreading of social education completely anymore, and whatever spreads will at least slow down the loss of social intellect.

The real opportunity these advanced communication technologies offer is that, social education programs of the highest quality and depth, preferably prepared by an Independent Institution as described above, can now be made freely available to all individuals through these e-channels without any limitations on teaching capacity. All that is required then is to make as many members of the society as possible to take these education programs. The situation is not as hopeless as it were in the previous decades anymore.

6.2 Social Awareness

Social Awareness And The Cheaters

Social education is necessary but not enough for rising and keeping social awareness. Social awareness requires the continuous process of spending time and effort to observe and understand the developments in economics and politics within and out of the society.

To be more precise, on top of social education, social awareness requires the fulfilment of two further conditions simultaneously. One is having access to complete and correct information on the developments in economics and politics, preferably by the individual himself, or in cases where that is not easy, at least by the experts. And the other is allocating the time and effort required for analysing the information, or at least for reviewing the analyses of the experts.

Any concentrated interest group willing to manipulate the society on a specific issue, whether in economics or politics, needs to make sure that the awareness of the society on that specific issue is weak or preferably non-existent. Therefore, it has to weaken the fulfilment of at least one, or preferably both of the conditions above.

Regarding the free flow of complete and correct information, many techniques that were discussed before can be utilized. These include censoring out vital information, and whenever this is not possible, crowding out vital information with too much noise or additional irrelevant information such that the information required for rational decision making can not be filtered out easily or quickly. And if the flow of information can not be prevented either, the next step is trying to distract the attention of the individuals away from social issues to matters of daily survival (like the need to work hard to earn a living) or entertainment (like offering many free choices of tv shows, internet games, social media etc), so that they will have limited time and effort left to be spent on developing awareness on economic and political issues.

And if none of the above is possible, the final step is to practically censor the genuine experts with goodwill, through crowding out the media with a huge supply of self-appointed or fake or simply bought-out experts.

Identifying The Genuine Experts

A society not listening to expert advice is destined to get lost somewhere sometime. But to start listening to the experts, the society first needs to find out the genuine experts who are both qualified to comment on the issue at hand, and only express their sincere and complete opinion. Reciprocally, in order to get trusted by the society again, the experts need to somehow reveal their ability and goodwill to the society. And finally, to embrace its critical social responsibility to facilitate the increase in the intellectual level of the society, the digital media has to develop ways to distinguish between qualified expert opinion and noise.

One simple way to achieve this can be through assigning a voluntary tag to each participant to be used with all communications in the digital media. If a participant desires, this tag will reveal three bits of information on himself. First, his true identity. Second, why he believes he has the qualification to comment on a certain issue, including his education and experience on the matter. And third, whether he has or ever had any material relation with any concentrated interest group or any economic entity related to the discussed issue. In case this tag is missing, the other participants will recognize that they are facing either an unqualified or a deliberately misguiding opinion, and thus should not trust its validity. This will at least serve to sort out genuine expert opinion for those who are in search for it.

For the declaration through this tag to make any sense, an independent institution should be formed and supervised by the Legislative Authority within the political system (the parliament or equivalent), such that it will assign these tags for those participants willing to have one and periodically validate all the information given there.

This approach will help to identify the genuine experts on a personal basis, but only for those who care to search for expertise. However, within the reality of daily practise, for keeping adequate social awareness for all the society, common sources of high-expertise that are much easier to locate through the digital media have to be introduced as well.

Independent Sources Of Information And Analysis

Within the jargon of the principal-agent relationship, a functioning democracy requires the society to act as a qualified principal, and that in turn requires its members to have adequate social education, experience and awareness. However, even if an individual has adequate social education and experience to start with, to keep his awareness, he still needs to spend significant time and effort continuously, both to reach a huge volume of information on local and global developments, and to analyse such information within a complex framework of causalities. In practise, although a few may manage this, such dedication of time and effort, and such development of expertise, is practically impossible for most of the society. The society, therefore, needs more efficient ways of increasing its awareness, namely reliable sources that will enable it to reach both the vital information and the analysis of that information easily. In short, the society, as the principal, needs information-gathering-and-analysing agents, whom it should be able to trust with their abilities and goodwill.

INDEPENDENT SOURCES OF INFORMATION

The first step in this agency relation is creating agents that will supply correct and complete information to the public.

Historically this function is supposed to be handled by the so-called free press. Unfortunately, free press is one of the worst degenerated concepts in practise. In this book, therefore, a different concept, namely *independent sources of information*, will be used and defined from scratch.

Independence naturally requires and therefore includes freedom, but it also necessitates not being controlled directly or indirectly by any concentrated interest group through financing or any other means, and not owing any favours to anybody.

Being a source of information, in our definition, means gathering information on economic, political and other relevant social issues and then supplying that information to the public. Thus, it is completely different from any sources of entertainment. Unfortunately, the thick red line in between disappears when the two merge incidentally or deliberately under the concept of free press, as they happen to use similar media. To clarify, being a newspaper, magazine, radio or TV or web channel, or any other sort of classic or digital platform, does not qualify as a source of information in this sense, unless it serves the function in the way defined above. Rather, most of these platforms are just sources of entertainment today, and that is fine in principle, even though their practical over-use serves as a distractor of attention from major social issues. The crucial observation is that, the widespread existence of sources of entertainment is no proof of the existence of independent sources of information within a society.

The society has to appreciate what independent sources of information really are and why they are vital for the proper functioning of democracy, and thus must heavily demand their existence.

INDEPENDENT SOURCES OF ANALYSIS

The second step is creating agents that will correctly and objectively analyse the raw information supplied, utilising their superior expertise, and present their conclusions to their principals, namely the whole society.

Historically this function is supposed to be handled by the economists and political analysts serving within the free press. Unfortunately, within today's complex structures covering a wide web of conflicts of interests, the objectivity of these experts may also be questioned, simply because keeping individual independence is getting impossibly difficult in practise within structures that are not independent themselves.

What the society actually needs are *independent sources of analysis*. To reemphasize, independence not only requires freedom, but also necessitates not being controlled directly or indirectly by any concentrated interest groups through financing or any other means, and not owing any favours to anybody.

The society should also appreciate that access to raw information alone is of very limited use unless there is access to objective expert analysis of that information, and thus must heavily demand the existence of these independent sources of analysis as well.

FINANCING AND INDEPENDENCE

Gathering and analysing information requires the employment of utmost expertise that does not come for free or even for cheap. And most of the times a team of experts must be working together within some sort of structure. This necessity naturally creates a major financing need for sources of both information and analysis.

In principle these sources are supposed to be the agents of the society, but in practise their financing needs are met by either private groups or advertising, rather than the society. Private financers have to be assumed to be profit oriented, either directly in cases where the agent can make profits, or worse, indirectly as the agent is made to serve the benefits of some concentrated interest groups hidden in the background, against the benefit of the society. Advertisers, whether private or governmental, expect not only direct benefits from such advertising, but also indirect benefits through practically preventing the agent from publishing anything against their interests.

Once these agents are defined to have a focus on social issues only, thus totally separate from any source of entertainment, their direct profitability for both the private financers and the advertisers vanish immediately. That leaves any private financers or advertisers with indirect motives only, meaning that the concentrated benefits of whoever is financing the agent in whatever ways are expected to be promoted by the agent over the interests of the society. And thus, independence of any such agents will practically be impossible.

This clarifies the crucial need for the public financing of the information-gathering-and-analysing agents of the society. Any intellectually-adult society can immediately see that it is not a bright move for a principal to make some concentrated interest groups pay directly or indirectly for its agent, while that agent is supposed to reveal the best interests of the principal against those concentrated interest groups.

EXPOSING THE SOCIETY TO A DIVERSITY OF OPINIONS

The existence of various independent sources of information and analysis, with different viewpoints and tendencies, will enable every individual to access a diversity of opinions beyond a single viewpoint. This will be a very valuable contribution to the quality of democracy, as once individuals break the boundaries that limit their communication only with those like themselves, and start to listen to or even communicate with those who have different opinions, they will also start to be more tolerant to alternative views and may even change their own opinion to embrace other viewpoints, moving them towards a more moderate and rational stand, away from the extremes.

HOW SHOULD THESE INDEPENDENT AGENTS BE FINANCED BY THE SOCIETY

Once the need for *absolute independence* and *diversity of opinion* for the sources of information and analysis is accepted, it becomes clear that the financing of these agents by the society should be based on objective rules that define which agents will be supported and how much support each should get.

In principle, as the society will be paying for the services of these agents, the society should make this decision. And in practise, this can be done in a fair way if the society utilizes the same democratic approach that it uses to elect the parties / representatives to the Legislative House, to determine the agents to be supported by public funds. This approach will enable the real independence of these agents from the Executive Authority (president, prime minister, government), and will promote the emergence of a diversity of opinions rather than having a similar set of agents all defending the same opinion.

For operational simplicity, this process of voting for the agents to be supported by the public can be done simultaneously with the elections for Legislation and Execution.

The first step of the process will be inviting the candidates for sources of information and sources of analysis, as two separate groups, to join the agent elections. For sources of information, the candidates will most probably be structured entities resembling news channels. For sources of analysis, candidates can have any structure from a team of experts to entities resembling major think tanks.

A crucial issue here is that, the voluntary personal tags defined in the previous sub-section must be mandatory for each and every team member of the candidate agent, to reveal his identity, education, experience and the non-existence of any potential conflicts of interest between the society and any other third parties that he may be in relation with. Furthermore, the agent as an entity should declare whether any team member who has worked for the agent in the past has developed any material relationship with any interest group within a certain period after leaving the agent (say a couple of years). This last bit of information will not effect the agent's candidacy, as such relations are not within the control of the agent, however, it will create a track record revealing the agent's ability and sincerity in choosing the right people for its team.

On the second step, at each election, in addition to voting for political candidates for the Legislation and the Execution, each voter can be given the right to choose, say, three agents for sources of information and three agents for sources of analysis, that he likes and prefers most.

On the third step, following each election, based on the total number of votes they get, the highest ranking 10 sources of information and 10 sources of analysis will be elected as the *outstanding agents* in their respective groups for the period until the next elections. Needless to say, having 10 agents in either group is just a rational rule of thumb, in the sense that it introduces enough variety without wasting public resources. Depending on the society and the prevailing circumstances this number may vary.

As the public funds to be allocated to the financing of these outstanding agents is practically limited, the distribution of these funds should be fair in the sense that, on the one hand each agent should get a minimum financing to ensure its survival and functionality, and on the other hand the more preferred ones should get paid more. Therefore, the financial support each agent will get in each group will be the sum of a fixed allocation for basic functionality plus a variable one based on the share of votes it got within its peer group in the election[17].

It is of utmost importance that, to assure complete independency, these outstanding agents will not accept any other financing from any other private interest group or governmental entity as long as they receive public financing. And all the information and analysis these outstanding agents supply will be completely accessible by the whole society, including those who have not voted for them.

BENEFITS OF THIS NEW PRINCIPAL-AGENT RELATION

The principal-agent relation structured in this way between the society, as the principal, and the independent sources of information and analysis, as the agents, will bring many benefits. First of all, the society will know the true identity, education and experience of the team within each agent. Second, the society will be sure of the financial independence of the agents and the non-existence (or at least the minimisation) of conflicts of interest. Third, each individual will know that all the information and analyses he reads are public and there is no tailor-made information based on his own digital footprint to manipulate his opinion. Fourth, each individual who wishes to listen to different opinions can easily access all the information gathering and analysis services provided by all these agents, knowing that he will be exposed to the most qualified commentators defending the alternate viewpoints. And finally, the ongoing relation between the society and its agents, based on the evaluation and re-election of the agents periodically, will motivate the agents to perform their best and develop a good track record for themselves based on their demonstrated expertise and goodwill.

TRACK RECORDS OF AGENTS FOR EXPERTISE AND INDEPENDENCE

If an agent, whether as an independent source of information or analysis, develops a successful track record in the dimensions of its ability and goodwill, the demand for its services will rise and it will increase its share of votes at each consecutive election, getting more and more financial support from public resources. Conversely, if an outstanding agent fails on one of the fronts, its support will weaken and eventually it will lose public financing. *This dynamic agency relation, with no interest group but only the public on the principal side, is necessary for the society to keep its social awareness high enough to run a well functioning democracy.*

Chapter 7 : VITAL IMPROVEMENTS IN DEMOCRACY

7.1   The Failure Of Democracy: Confusing The Means And The Ends

From the viewpoint of economics, creating a fair balance between an individual's contribution to the society and the compensation he gets in return is vital for the well functioning of the system, and for that purpose Free Market Economy is indispensable. The dynamics of supply and demand, based on free competition, bring out an equilibrium that is supposed to create this fair balance, and such fairness makes the existence of economic inequality acceptable up to some rational extent. However, in cases of weak or mis regulation, free competition eventually creates too much concentration of power and too much inequality, destroying the fairness of the system.

Keeping that risk in mind, the current western social order was so designed that, the economic system based on free markets will be checked and balanced by the political system based on Democracy. As Democracy is based on absolute equality, in the sense that each individual has one and only one vote, it is supposed to counter act to cure any excessive rise in economic inequality and / or any over-concentration of power within the social order.

Under such a check-and-balance structure, it follows by definition that, if things are persistently going terribly wrong in the economy, then something has to be going wrong in the political system.

In other words, in the western social order based on Free Market Economy and Democracy, the causation starts in politics and follows in economics, although the end-effects are observed the other way round.

In light of this observation, *at times of long lasting widespread problems in the economy, what needs to be done first is to diagnose the trouble in Democracy and improve the system to overcome those deadlocks, such that the political system restarts to function properly. The recovery of the economic system will then follow naturally.*

THE SOURCE OF THE TROUBLE: PRINCIPLES OR PRACTISE

There may be several reasons behind the malfunctioning of Democracy. The basic principles of Democracy might have become outdated, or they may be mis-applied unknowingly or deliberately, or both. And in today's case in the western societies, unfortunately, the answer is both.

Therefore, the first step to be taken is to re-think and re-define the principles of the democratic system such that they can fit the conditions of the 21st century and beyond. And the next step is to make sure that these new principles are applied to practise properly. And for the second step to work, it is crucial that the new principles should be applicable to practise without losing their soul, since ideal-but-inapplicable principles can not cure any troubles.

THE MEANS AND THE ENDS

As the economic and political complexity of the globally integrating world is increasing over time, there is no choice but to improve the democratic system such that the societies can still guard their interests and maximise their welfare. This improvement process has to start with the realization that the means utilised in a democratic system are there to serve the purpose of reaching the targeted ends, and thus their reason of existence is justified if and only if the desired ends are reached.

The targeted end to be achieved in a Democracy is guarding the interests of the society and maximising its welfare in the long-term, while respecting each and every individual's rights and freedoms as much as possible. This end is supposed to be achieved through a representative relationship, where the society, as the principal, elects the politicians with the required ability and goodwill, as its agents, and keeps these agents accountable through proper and periodic evaluation, namely elections, and replaces them with better ones whenever necessary.

However, when the society is practically incapable of either electing the right agents or evaluating them properly afterwards (meaning a practical loss of accountability for the agent and thus a loss of legitimacy for the political system), the outcome is a decline in the welfare of the society, commonly coupled with some loss of individual rights and freedoms, and the ends are lost. In such cases, keeping the means, namely the election system, intact, is of no use for the society but just remains to be an artificial makeup on the surface.

Therefore, in almost all democracies today, *the failure of the means of the system has to be questioned and the necessary improvements to embrace the necessities of our day have to be made, without prejudice.*

7.2   The Licence To Vote

Social Responsibility And The Need For Preconditions For Voting

Everybody has the right and the freedom to drive a car. And everybody pays with their taxes for the roads and bridges built for driving. However, one still can not be permitted to drive a car unless he gets a driver's licence which is based on a basic education on driving, making sure that he is qualified enough to drive. The reason is simple: without the education to get a license, one may harm the others in the society if he tries to drive a car, and the others have a right to travel safely, thus limiting his freedom-to-drive-without-a-licence. And there is no problem with the precondition of a licence for driving, simply because everybody has the freedom and the right and a fair opportunity to get a licence if they desire. And once an individual gets a licence, he can drive wherever he wants.

Similarly, *in a democracy, an individual's basic freedom and right to vote without being subject to any preconditions (like having some capability of understanding the relevant basic issues), is limited by the right of the society to be governed well to increase its long-term welfare.* In other words, other people's right to be governed by political agents with ability and goodwill, makes each voter responsible for both making and keeping himself capable enough to elect and to evaluate agents properly. The easiest and fastest way to gain such capability is to get some social education, and the proof of such capability will be a *Licence to Vote*, to be obtained by completing the education. Once an individual gets his licence, he is free to vote in any way he desires.

THE OBJECTIONS…

There are many common and strong arguments saying that the right to vote should come without any preconditions, that is to say without the need for any social education and Licence, because

- individuals are *born to be citizens*, meaning that they should have the unconditional right to vote without any need to bother for further personal development,

or

- individuals are *made to pay taxes*, and there can be no taxation without political representation associated with an unconditional right to vote,

or

- individuals are *bound by the laws of the society*, which gives them the right to be politically represented with an unconditional right to vote.

… ARE RATHER SUPPORTIVE

All these arguments, based on individuals' rights, definitely have a touch of validity. However, the desire to have an unconditional right to vote still conflicts with the society's right to be governed well, and individuals' rights can not be (mis)used to harm the society.

Moreover, *the requirement to obtain a Licence to Vote through taking some social education does not contradict with any of the individuals' rights.* Just on the contrary, *increasing an individual's capability to understand economic and political issues better and thus to make better political choices, will let him get a higher return for the taxes he pays and be governed by better laws, both of which will increase his own welfare as well as that of the society.*

The Right To Vote

In a Democracy, the right to vote is believed to be sacred. This does not mean that it has to be an unconditional birth-right. Just on the contrary, *the right to vote has to be earned* through fulfilling certain preconditions, *provided that each and every individual is given a fair opportunity to earn the right to vote.*

Societies naturally and rationally fear of a black scenario where an individual can be practically denied a fair opportunity to earn the right to vote, in case any preconditions are attached. Thus they have settled for a dark-grey scenario where the right to vote is given as an unconditional birth-right, without any need to earn it. Unfortunately, that approach has now become irrational as a means, as it became inadequate in reaching the desired ends in today's complex world. Therefore, now is the time to advance towards a better scenario, where everybody will definitely be given a fair opportunity, not only in principle but also in practise, and are expected to earn the right to vote, but this time enabling the economic and political systems to function as desired. And therefore, now is the time to accept that *the real sacred value is and must be "to have the right to be given a fair opportunity to earn the right to vote", rather than a simple unconditional birth-right to vote.*

To earn the right to vote, and thus to act as a principal in the democratic system, an individual first has to become capable of properly evaluating the agents and their policies, so that the accountability of the agent, which is at the heart of the legitimacy of the democratic system, will have a practical meaning. That, in turn, requires the completion of a social education program by the individual.

Licence To Vote Based On Social Education As A Primary Precondition

For democracies to survive in today's complex social, economic and political environment, one necessary condition is the voters' capability to elect and to evaluate the political agents properly. The voters have to demonstrate this capability through getting a Licence to Vote by completing a social education program, prepared by an Independent Institution (under the supervision of the Legislative Authority within the political system), as described in Section 6.1.

Such a program, by its nature, has to be free, meaning that it has to be financed by the state, and easily accessible through both classic classroom education and online technologies. Actually, it is much better to utilize today's advanced online communication technologies, as the content offered through e-media can be standardized and therefore every individual will go through exactly the same highest quality education material. Classic class room approach should only be used for the older generations who may not be familiar with the newest technologies.

After completion of the social education program, the verification of adequate understanding of the covered material should be made through a reliable examination process that prevents cheating of any sort, and then a life-long Licence to Vote will be issued. The examination techniques developed by universities during the 2019 pandemic can be further developed to enable fair and reliable examination on an individual basis at public e-examination centres designed solely for that purpose, where each individual will go through a fully automated standard exam process, under exactly the same conditions with every other individual. And the exams can be evaluated by algorithms without any human intervention, to make sure that no subjective judgement takes place and thus the results are perfectly fair.

THE TIMING OF SOCIAL EDUCATION

For the coming generations, such a one-year program (as discussed in Section 6.1) can be integrated to the very end of their professional education, following the latest academic degree an individual will attain, and thus before they start their active work life, in order not to cause any interruptions afterwards. This will practically correspond to sometime between ages 18 to 25, when the learning capability of each individual is at its maximum and his interest in economic and political issues has adequately developed.

For those who are already in their active work life, between the ages 25 to 60, having a one year interruption may practically be impossible. Those individuals can initially be given a temporary Licence to Vote, just for once, say for five years, during which they can vote without the requirement of completing any education. Within that period, they should be expected to complete the social education program, say through weekend courses or online. And in case they do not bother to do so, they will lose their right to vote by the end of the fifth year, until they complete the program sometime afterwards.

Finally, for those above the age 60 at the date of the establishment of the licence requirement, the program should only be optional, and they will keep their right to vote without the precondition of social education.

The Duty To Stay Aware

Getting the Licence to Vote is only the first step of fulfilling the responsibility of the individual as a voter.

Once an individual completes the social education program and earns his right to vote, it then becomes his duty to stay aware of the developments around, locally and globally, so that he can remain to be capable of evaluating the politicians and their policies. Otherwise, the means will once again fail to lead to the desired ends: if, once they get their Licence to Vote, individuals exercise their right to vote without fulfilling their duty to stay aware, the precondition and all the effort made to satisfy it, will be mostly wasted. And then it will again be just a wishful dream for the society to have sustainable development to maximise its welfare, or even to live in a stable social order.

Further Potential Preconditions For The License To Vote

The intellectual level and the social awareness of the society is the foremost precondition for the proper functioning of Democracy, thus the need for a Licence to Vote based on the requirement of social education is clear. That, however, may not be the only precondition, and there are others discussed in the political literature. Two other candidates for becoming additional preconditions are the contribution of the individual to the society and the mental health of the individual.

CONTRIBUTION TO THE SOCIETY

A widely debated principle in politics is that there should be no taxation without representation, meaning that if an individual has no right to vote, then the state (thus the society) has no right to tax that individual. This is based on the argument that any individual who pays taxes must have the right to reflect his opinion on how those taxes will be spent. And the opposing argument says that even if an individual has no right to vote, he still enjoys the social environment (including the economic and political system with all their advantages) in the society and thus he has to contribute to the financing of that social order.

Utilising similar arguments, the reverse can also be debated, with even a stronger logic: if an individual has no contribution to the society, revealed by the fact that he is not paying any taxes and has never paid much of a tax, while still enjoying the social environment, then that individual should have no right to get represented in the political decision making process, practically meaning that he should not have the right to vote.

Therefore, another candidate for becoming a precondition for getting the Licence to Vote may be the contribution of the individual to the society, which can be proven through paying taxes, as any individual who creates some value for the society somehow gets paid for it and consequently pays taxes. However, for such a precondition to exist without contradicting fairness, and thus be rationally acceptable, the society should first be able to make sure that each and every individual is given a fair opportunity to get a proper education and employment afterwards. Only under the condition of fairness of opportunity, a society may have the right to demand contribution as a precondition for having the right to vote.

In a society where every individual is really given a fair opportunity to make a contribution to the society, the demand for such a precondition will make sense. In that case, the precondition may require that an individual, or at least one of those in a couple, is either paying taxes currently, or had paid taxes beforehand that sum up to a certain time period and/or an aggregate amount. Needless to say, the taxes that count here should only be those that reflect a contribution to the society, like income taxes, and not the irrelevant ones like consumption taxes.

To reemphasize, unless a fair opportunity can be given to each and every individual to make a contribution to the society, such a precondition can not be acceptable.

MENTAL HEALTH

While discussing the intellect and the social awareness of an individual, the natural hidden assumption is that the individual has mental health. In cases where an individual is medically diagnosed for mental illness, the right to vote does not have a meaning by definition. These cases, however, were rare, at least until the recent decades, and thus were ignored for practical purposes.

The real trouble is that, mental health, which is generally fine during most of the life on an individual, can be lost by ageing. As societies get ever older, such cases may reach a considerable proportion within the society and may eventually harm the democratic system, as some within the elderly may lose their once-perfect ability to observe and evaluate the developments around and thus their awareness, eventually losing their capability to vote rationally, while they will already have a Licence to Vote received beforehand. Therefore, there may be a need for another precondition which should be checked periodically to validate the continuation of the licence.

One practical way of applying such a precondition, can be to require all the individuals beyond a certain age, say the average lifespan of the society plus five years, to take a medical examination periodically, say once in every three years, to certify that there is no obstacle in their mental health to prevent them from rational thinking and thus maintaining their awareness.

Accepting The Undeniable

In an ideal society, where all the individuals in the society educate themselves on social matters willingly and keep themselves aware ever after, and can get some professional education to enable them to make a contribution to the society, and will stay mentally healthy till the very last day of their lives, there would have been no need for any preconditions for having the right to vote. Unfortunately, no society is or will ever be anywhere close to that ideal. And keeping a closed eye to this fact will not save any society.

Mandatory social education and the Licence to Vote are the minimum vital changes required for the political system to regain its functionality. The other potential preconditions need to be debated further.

And in the social education front, there is more to be done.

7.3   The Licence To Govern

Improving Democracy (I): Politics Must Become A Profession

Once it is realized that the political system is the most critical component of the social order in a society, it naturally follows that becoming a politician can not be left to the ancient and naïve anyone-can-do-it principle. Just on the contrary, *politics must be the most important and the most respected profession in the society, which requires some specific education and expertise of its own*, that neither comes naturally nor through any other type of professional education or expertise.

LICENSE TO GOVERN

A society that accepts the need for a Licence to Vote for all its members as the principals, should naturally demand a further licence for all those aspiring to be the political agents. Such a high level licence, which may be called the *Licence to Govern*, should be mandatory for all those who would like to be elected to posts in Legislation and Execution, and for all those who will serve at all sorts of top levels of government and bureaucracy within the state.

The Licence to Govern will still be based on social education, but this time targeting a high level of expertise, and thus will take a longer time to complete[18]. The basic principles, however, will practically be the same: the education and the examination will be organized and the licences will be granted by the same Independent Institution that handles the Licences to Vote, totally free of charge for any individual willing to participate in the program, whenever he wants. Once again, it is crucial that, each and every individual in the society, must have a fair opportunity to receive such high level social education and get the Licence to Govern, subject to the same rational conditions as everybody else.

And just like the right to be given a fair opportunity to earn the right to vote regarding the principals, there is a corresponding sacred value, namely "*the right to be given a fair opportunity to earn the right to govern*" for all those who aspire to become political agents. And again it is the society's duty and responsibility to guard this sacred value.

BUT POLITICS NEED NOT BE THE ONLY PROFESSION

Although politics must be a profession on its own, it does not have to be the only profession of the individual, simply because there is not much of a job security in politics – at least in democracies. Actually, it may even be better for politicians to be multi-professional, that is to say to have some experience in other professions, as they will be better connected to the realities of practical life, and have diverse backgrounds that will enable better decision making in both the Legislation and the Execution. All that is needed is a complete transparency on their involvement with other professions, so that the society can decide whether there can be any potential conflicts of interest or not.

Improving Democracy (II): The Society Needs To Pay For Good Governance

In the ideal democracy in the dreams of the ancient Greek philosophers, the society grants the honour of serving the society to its best fit members, who, in turn, with their infinite wisdom and endless goodwill, sacrifice their own being for the best interests of the society. Although they had such sky-high expectations in principle, these philosophers neither lacked any wisdom nor lost their senses to hear and see, thus they were very well aware, and thus explicitly warned all future societies, that such expectations may be utterly unrealistic in practical life. However, as if that were not the case, most societies, even in the 21st century, still seem to have the expectation of finding such politicians, with infinite wisdom and goodwill, but without any material and moral expectations in return, apart from the honour of sacrificing themselves, to represent and to serve the society. It may be better for every society to cease such unrealistic expectations and face the reality.

As discussed in Section 4.5, societies now need politicians with much superior ability, coupled with permanent goodwill, and that requires satisfying the politicians' moral and material needs as good as, or preferably better, than the private sector can. Unfortunately, most societies will be irritated by the idea that the politicians and the bureaucrats should be paid as generously as their equivalent talents in the private sector. And thus, as principals, they are doomed to choose among agents who are either incapable of protecting the interests of the society against those talented ones who represent the concentrated interests of some economic entities, or worse, who will be easy preys for corruption.

The right path a society should take is, on the one hand providing competitive compensation to attract top talent to politics and bureaucracy, while on the other hand requiring utmost transparency to deter such talent from corruption. And transparency is not that difficult to achieve, if the society really demands it.

Improving Democracy (III): Introducing Ethics Codes In Politics

Once politics is turned into a profession requiring a separate licence, and the society starts to compensate its agents, namely the politicians, competitively and fairly, the final step will be establishing transparency.

When politicians are considered individually, transparency requires a legally binding declaration of any material relations in the past and the present, with any economic or other concentrated interest groups, from both the candidates and the politicians currently on duty.

Such transparency will ensure two things in principle. First, any politician who already has contradictory interests of his own against the society may not be elected. And second, any politician who explicitly, practically meaning foolishly, develops any relations with any interest groups during his time on duty such that contradictory interests arise, may not be elected ever again. Unfortunately, in practice, Cheaters are sophisticated creators of corruption, and any favours done by any politician on duty for any concentrated interest group will usually be compensated after the politician leaves his political position in due time. Thus, such transparency on an individual basis will not be enough to guard the society against corruption.

This is where political parties step in to play a vital role. Contrary to any individual politician, political parties have, at least in principle, a long life in the political arena. The society, as the principal, may use this difference in lifespans to its advantage and develop a two step transparency requirement for political parties.

As a first step each political party should be made to declare any material relations in the past and present, with any economic or other concentrated interest groups, of its first time or returning candidates, of its members on political duty, and of its upper management. This is the party-level equivalent of the declaration of the individual candidates or politicians.

As a second step, *each political party should be made to declare any material relations developed with any concentrated interest groups, of the politicians who were previously elected to the legislative or the executive posts under that party, within a certain period (say a couple of years) after they have left their active duties* or ceased to become candidates in later elections.

This second step of transparency will create a track record for the political party based on the ethical track records of the ex-politicians who have been the candidates or elected representatives of that party in the past. And that track record will be one of the most valuable assets of any political party, as it will enable the party to endorse the ethical values of any future politicians during their candidacy, in the eye of the society. From the viewpoint of the society, the better the track record of the party, the more the society will believe in the goodwill of its candidates and thus be inclined to elect them to duty.

From the viewpoint of the candidate politicians, the better the track record of the party, the more it will attract the candidates with superior capabilities and high moral values, as these candidates will know that their career will not be stained and wasted within a crowd of unethical agents. And that in turn will enable the party to choose its eventual candidates from a wider and better pool of candidates-for-candidacy. This chicken and egg relation will in time create stronger political party images for the parties who do a good job of selecting capable and ethical candidates. Eventually the political arena will cease to be a lemons market and will start to attract ever better candidates for the political agency service to the society.

CONCLUSION

GUARDING THE ECONOMIC AND POLITICAL SYSTEMS NECESSITATES IMPROVING THEM

Free Market Economy and Democracy, when designed and applied properly, can create a fine system of checks and balances, and promote the best interests of the society. In this regard, they should be highly valued and heavily guarded by each and every member of the society. But no system can be the absolute best solution for all times and conditions, and thus these systems have to be continuously improved as times change, to compensate for their emerging weaknesses, to update their principles to fit to the changing structure and demands of the society, and to cure their misapplications, and thus to sustain their stability and success. But if the society just takes these economic and political systems for granted, and not only fails to value and guard them, but also fails to improve them, the systems that once upon a time served well in principle and achieved success in practise, will eventually become outdated and thus open to deliberate misapplication of their principles to serve some concentrated interests rather than the society.

THE TROUBLE WITH WEAKENING SOCIAL INTELLECT

Each individual in the society is expected to play a vital role in the economy as a consumer and in politics as a voter. Therefore, societies need to realize that their economic system based on Free Markets and their political system based on Democracy can not function optimally, or even satisfactorily, unless the average Social Intellect of the society is above a certain threshold. And that threshold is rising every passing day.

If the rise in this threshold, namely the pace of change in the complexity of the economic, political and social environment, is faster than the increase in the intellectual level of the society, the Social Intellect of the society starts to fall in relative terms.

The society then loses the ability to understand the economic and political environment, and becomes open to be manipulated to make choices that transfer economic and political power to concentrated interest groups who serve their own interests at the expense of the society. And Free Market Economy and Democracy start to fail to serve their functions.

The society must cure such weakening of Social Intellect and try to attain social awareness before the trouble with its economic and political systems pass the point of no return.

ECONOMICS CAN NOT BE CURED UNLESS POLITICS IS

Concentration and monopolization of economic power is in the nature of free markets when left to their own devices. And such economic power will eventually acquire some direct or indirect means of political power. The maximisation of the society's welfare, however, requires preventing the build up of any kind of concentration of power in either economics or politics. And that in turn requires the society to demand and get it accomplished through the political system. Therefore, for the economic system to work properly, first the political system must be working properly.

Reading backwards, if the political system fails, the economic system has no choice but to fail sooner or later. The trouble is that, the failure of the political system usually goes unnoticed until the failure of the economic system becomes clear. Even worse, in most cases, the society falls short of realising that if something has gone wrong with economics, most probably something has been going wrong with politics way before that, and that the economic system can not be cured unless the political system is cured first. Unfortunately, societies are still wasting precious time in search for cures for their economic system while neglecting the major structural problems of their political system.

RISING SOCIAL INTELLECT IS THE KEY

Having the right to decide one's own future in a Democracy is a great feeling, however, if done without having the necessary intellectual background, it ends up in selecting the wrong future. The only solution, although not a quick and easy one, is to increase the overall Social Intellect of the society.

Once the society cures its weakening Social Intellect and attains sufficient level of social awareness, Free Market Economy and Democracy can be treated for their existing ills, both in principle and in practise, and will become the best systems among all the currently available options.

THE AUTHOR

Salih Reisoglu has served as the CEO of an Investment Management Company for 20 years, and is an expert on Capital Markets with over 30 years of experience in analysing economics and politics. He is a regular guest speaker on many TV channels and universities. He holds an MSc in Computer Engineering from Lehigh University, and an MBA in Finance from the Wharton School of the University of Pennsylvania.

INDEX OF KEY CONCEPTS

ENDNOTES

[1]   Social Intellect is one of the many topics discussed in an integrated fashion in my book Missing Intellect in Economics and Politics. In Book One of this series it is presented in a different flow and structure, to clarify all relevant issues better.

[2]   Welfare is not solely based on wealth, but also on the distribution of wealth within the society, i.e. inequality. The concept of welfare, and dynamics of change in welfare, will be discussed in detail in Book Three of this series.

[3]   REGULATION FOR PROTECTING AND PROMOTING THE SOCIETY'S INTEREST

To clarify further, this principle argues that the outcome of the competition in the market should at least not harm the society, preferably create value for the society, and at best maximise the value created for the society. Therefore, the society, through its political agents, namely the Legislative and Executive Bodies within the political system, must set the rules and enact regulations such that the society not only wins as a result of the competition defined by those rules and regulations, but also maximises its benefit from that competition.

The violation of this principle hurts the society most when there are negative side effects, called *externalities* in the economic jargon.

Even when the producers and consumers are both happy with the functioning of the market, the outcome may still not be beneficial for the society at large. This happens when the transaction they agree to execute may have negative consequences that effect some third parties within the society who are not on either side of the transaction. This practically means that these third parties are unwillingly incurring a cost because of that transaction which actually should have been paid by one or both of the sides taking part in the transaction.

One very well known and fashionable example of externalities is global warming, in which as a result of the production techniques utilized by the producers of certain goods, which the consumers are happily consuming, the whole global society is suffering. Unfortunately, many other externalities generated by various economic activities are not that well recognized, and thus the society pays a price without being aware of it. Therefore, it is the duty of the regulator, as an agent of the society, to detect and prevent the emergence of such externalities, and in cases where they are inevitable, at least make sure through proper regulation that the sides to the relevant transaction carry the full costs of these externalities, rather than the society.

[4] In mathematical terms, if $A + B = C$ (where A, B, C are all positive numbers), and if A is increasing while C is decreasing, then the decrease in B has to be larger than the increase in A. In our case, the increase in A corresponds to the increase in the cheaters' benefits, and the decrease in C corresponds to the decrease in the overall welfare of the society. And the decrease in B corresponds to the decrease in the welfare of the rest of the society. It then follows that, the decrease in the welfare of the rest of the society has to be larger than the increase in the cheaters' benefits.

[5] Called the Lemons Theory in the economics jargon, as the process was initially illustrated utilizing the used cars market, and used cars are called Lemons.

[6] Determining the frequency of the performance assessments is another troublesome issue regarding the agency relation. On the one hand, the assessment should be done in shorter terms, to be sure that there is no depreciation of the agent's goodwill due to being left unchecked for long

periods of time, and there is no depreciation of the agent's abilities due to his failure to adjust to the changing conditions in the environment. On the other hand, as the agent carries the risk of losing his agency after each assessment, the time horizon of the agent is actually the period between the assessments. Therefore, too frequent assessments will make it extremely difficult to align the interests of the agent with the long-term interests of the principal even when the agent is sincere.

[7] THE SELF CONFIDENCE OF THE INTELLECTUALLY CHILDREN
The well-known Dunning-Kruger Cognitive Bias in psychology literature fits well to the intellectually-children in our jargon. Applied to our analysis, it explains that the intellectually-children terribly over-estimate their intellectual level in issues that they know nothing about. The wide-spread social networks of our day, by letting people gather with others of their own kind, which in turn serves to confirm their misbeliefs with each others', makes this effect even stronger.

[8] In parliamentary democracies, there may be other minor political parties in the political arena, however, they may at best have a marginal effect on policy making even if they happen to be included in a coalition.

[9] As will be discussed in detail in Book Three of this series, Welfare is not a direct function of Wealth, but rather a combined outcome of Wealth and Inequality within a society. Welfare may actually be decreasing while Wealth is increasing in case there is an excessive increase in Inequality.

[10] The term Younger Generations refers to young adults, not children or teenagers.

[11] Some outstanding works include "Political Order and Political Decay" by Francis Fukuyama; and "Why Nations Fail" and "The Narrow Corridor" by Daron Acemoglu and James Robinson.

---

¹² Please refer to the works of Richard Thaler, including "Misbehaving" and "Nudge".

¹³ Correlation is a statistical relationship that shows how two or more variables change in relation to each other. Such a change does not necessarily show that there is some sort of causation relation between them – there may or may not be one. Therefore, revealing correlations is a valuable tool for social analysis, as a predictive relationship is revealed without the need to answer the difficult question of whether a causation relation exists and why.

¹⁴ For a detailed discussion on the topic, please refer to the periodical *Knowledge@Wharton*, dated Oct 11, 2018, for the article by Eric K. Clemons, "How Private Information Helps Fake News Fool the Public".

¹⁵ For a detailed discussion on the topic, please refer to the periodical *Knowledge@Wharton*, dated Jan 17, 2014, for the article by Tom Nichols, "The Death of Expertise".

¹⁶ When the purpose is manipulation of opinion, rather than spreading correct and complete information, concentrated interest groups and the Cheating Elite coincide.

¹⁷ In the allocation of public funds within each group, the share of each outstanding agent can be calculated on a fixed share plus a variable share basis.

The fixed share is the minimum amount of financing required to ensure an agent's survival and functionality. The variable share is the share of each outstanding agent within a predetermined total allocation. To be fair, the variable share has to be based on the proportion of the percentage of votes an outstanding agent got to the total percentage of votes all the outstanding agents got together.

To illustrate simply, let the 10 outstanding agents in the sources of information group are { A1, A2, … A10 }, with the corresponding votes {A1%, A2%, …. A10%}. Assume that each outstanding agent will get a fixed allocation of say 10 units, and there is a budget of 200 units for variable distribution.

Therefore, the total amount funds to be allocated to agent A2 will be:

Total financing for A2 =

> = [Fixed allocation per agent] + [Variable allocation for A2]
> = [10 units] + [A2% / (A1% + A2% + … + A10%) x 200 units]

[18] Some economically advanced societies have established systems whose functions resemble the higher level social education defined here, targeting to educate potential politicians or bureaucrats. One example is the Ecole Nationale d'Administration (ENA) in France that aims to train the politicians of the future. Another example can be the system in Singapore that tries to attract and educate those with the highest talent for politics or public service. But such examples are rare.

Printed in Great Britain
by Amazon

46455753R00116